KITCHEN GLASSWARE
of the Depression Years

By Gene Florence

Coordinated By Margaret Whitmyer

COLLECTOR BOOKS
P.O. Box 3009
Paducah, Kentucky 42001

The current values in this book should be used only as a guide. They are not intended to set prices, which vary from one section of the country to another. Auction prices as well as dealer prices vary greatly and are affected by condition as well as demand. Neither the Author nor the Publisher assumes responsibility for any losses that might be incurred as a result of consulting this guide.

Additional copies of this book may be ordered from:

COLLECTOR BOOKS
P.O. Box 3009
Paducah, Kentucky 42001
or
Gene Florence
P.O. Box 22186
Lexington, Kentucky 40522

@$17.95 Add $1.00 for postage and handling.

Copyright: Bill Schroeder, Gene Florence, 1981
ISBN: 0-89145-170-6

Printed by IMAGE GRAPHICS, Paducah, Kentucky

ABOUT THE AUTHOR

Gene Florence, born in Lexington in 1944, graduated from the University of Kentucky where he held a double major in mathematics and English. He taught nine years in the Kentucky school systems at the Junior High and High School levels before his glass collecting "hobby" became his full time job.

Mr. Florence has been interested in "collecting" since childhood, beginning with baseball cards and progressing through comic books, coins, bottles and finally, glassware. He first became interested in Depression glassware after purchasing a set of Sharon dinnerware at a garage sale for $5.00.

He has written several books on glassware: *The Collector's Encyclopedia of Depression Glass*, now in its fourth edition; *The Collector's Encyclopedia of Akro Agate; The Collector's Encyclopedia of Occupied Japan*, Volume I and II and the *Pocket Guide to Depression Glass*, now in its second edition.

Should you be in Lexington, he is often found at Grannie Bear Antique Shop located at 120 Clay Avenue. This is the shop he helped his mother set up in what was formerly her children's day care center. The shop derived its name from the term of endearment the toddlers gave her.

Should you know of any unlisted or unusual pieces of kitchenware of the type mentioned in this book, you may write him at Box 22186, Lexington, KY 40522. If you expect a reply, you must enclose a self addressed, stamped envelope --- and be patient. His travels and research often cause the hundreds of letters he receives weekly to backlog. He does appreciate your interest, however, and spends many hours answering your letters when time and circumstances permit.

ACKNOWLEDGEMENTS

The major acknowledgement in this book goes to Margaret Whitmeyer and her husband, Kenn; they traveled many miles gathering for me the majority of glass shown herein; and then they gave unstintingly of themselves in helping to organize it and set it up during the long, long hours of the photography sessions; they helped wrap and unwrap, clean and measure pieces; they allowed me to pick their brains and to make use of their longer experience and expertise in this particular field of collecting, i.e., Depression kitchenware. They believed in the need for a book of this type and pushed themselves and me to make it a reality.

A special thanks to my family, Cathy, my wife, for typing and editing my book and "chicken scratch" handwriting and to Chad, Marc, Mom, Dad, Sib, Charles, and Marie who must all carry the extra load at home while I'm out gathering information, glass, prices, etc.

Glassware and information came from the following persons: Nancy Maben, Charles and Sibyl Gaines, Gene and Gladys Florence, Michel Rosewitz, Joe and Florence Solito, Dee Long, and Jo Cunningham.

I'm especially grateful for the gracious reception and help given me by Lloyd Thrush and Philip Bee of the Anchor Hocking Glass Company. Too, I need to thank nameless people in their photography lab who reproduced copies of their old catalogues for my use.

As always, there are countless people behind a book who contribute to its conception either directly or indirectly. I'm very appreciative of all these people from the gatherers to the printers.

INDEX

FOREWARD

Kitchenware items from the Depression Era have never been more avidly collected than now. Everywhere I've traveled in the last few years I've heard the question, "When is someone going to write a book on kitchen items?" At first, though I knew my wife had bought some from time to time, I wasn't very interested. Yet, as I began to see the items turning up at shows and flea markets and had various persons question me about prices and manufacturers, etc., I became convinced there was truly a need for a book of this type. I can't tell you the hours that have gone into deciding how to set up a book in a manner that would be workable. Having now finished the book, there are some things I would've changed had I to do it again; yet, basically, I'm satisfied that this is, indeed, a workable format.

The items shown and priced in this book make up only a fraction of those available; but I am hopeful that through study of the items herein, you should be able to get an idea of the value of something you own or find on the market. We tried to obtain a representative sampling of the various types of glass kitchen items which were available to consumers at that time.

As in any collectible, there has to be a demand for prices to be established for a product. Kitchenware is only in its infant stages of collectibility now; therefore, I would expect there to be a steady rise in prices for the common items over the next years. In the short two years I've been studying these wares, the rarer items have already escalated, particularly in the area of reamers.

PRICING

All prices in this book are retail prices for mint condition glassware. This book is intended to be only a guide to prices as there are still some regional differences due to glass being more readily available in some areas than in others.

A price range has been given to the kitchenware items, however, **to allow for some wear and a little roughness** that is normally not allowed in other forms of Depression Glass. Remember, these were utilitarian items and were probably in use for years; therefore, kitchenware collectors will allow some roughness. This does not mean that cracks, chunks and chips are acceptable. To the contrary, these greatly reduce the value of a piece. It simply means that kitchenware collectors are a "hair" more lenient about the condition of the glassware than are collectors of Depression dinnerware; they have to be simply because most of the kitchenware doesn't exist in absolutely mint condition!

I have attempted to price the items by what the piece has actually been sold for and not by the "hoped for" prices. I have seen both higher and lower prices for most of the items shown; however, except for some few items that seem unique, prices are those which collectors have been willing to pay.

COLORS

Anytime the word green or pink occurs, it means a transparent (see through) color. Other color terms are described below.

Amethyst	a transparent, violet color
Black amethyst	color appears black but will show purple under a strong light
Blue	"Chalaine", an opaque, sky blue made by McKee cobalt, a transparent, dark blue "Delphite", an opaque, medium blue made by Jeannette
Clambroth	translucent off white
Custard	an opaque beige
Green	"Jad-ite", an opaque green made by Hocking "Jadite", an opaque green made by Jeannette "Skokie", an opaque green made by McKee
White	milk white milk glass all these terms simply indicate a white color opal white Vitrock, a white made by Hocking
Yellow	Vaseline, a transparent yellow "Seville" yellow, an opaque yellow made by McKee

PART 1
CRISSCROSS, HAZEL ATLAS COMPANY, 1936-1938

Collectors of Depression era kitchenware have continued the attitude of collecting sets of Depression Glass where possible. There are few sets per se available in kitchenware; so, there is great demand for those items that do constitute part of a set. Crisscross fits the "set" category admirably plus having the added feature of being found in cobalt blue which is a highly prized color. The most difficult items to find are the blue pitcher and the orange juice reamers in pink and blue.

	Blue	Crystal	Green	Pink
Bottle, water, 32 oz.	----	1.25- 1.50	----	----
Bottle, water, 64 oz.	----	2.50- 3.50	----	----
*Bowl, mixing, 6¾"	6.00- 7.50	1.00- 1.25	3.00- 4.00	4.00- 5.00
Bowl, mixing, 7¾"	8.00- 10.00	1.25- 1.50	4.00- 5.00	6.00- 7.50
Bowl, mixing, 8¾"	10.00- 12.50	2.00- 2.50	5.00- 6.00	8.00- 10.00
Bowl, mixing, 9¾"	12.50- 15.00	2.50- 3.00	7.00- 8.00	10.00- 12.00
Butter, ¼ lb.	15.00- 20.00	3.00- 5.00	**6.00- 8.00	8.00- 10.00
Butter, I lb.	30.00- 32.50	4.00- 5.00	15.00-17.50	22.00- 25.00
Creamer	----	1.50- 2.00	----	----
Pitcher, 54 oz.	75.00- 80.00	15.00-20.00	----	----
Reamer, lemon	65.00- 75.00	2.00- 3.00	6.00- 7.00	----
Reamer, orange	100.00-125.00	2.00- 3.00	6.00- 7.00	125.00-150.00
Refrigerator bowl, round, 5½" w/cover	----	2.00- 3.00	----	7.50- 8.50
Refrigerator bowl, w/cover				
4"x4"	7.50- 8.50	1.00- 2.00	4.00- 5.00	6.00- 7.50
4"x8"	12.50- 15.00	1.50- 2.00	7.00- 8.00	10.00- 12.50
8"x8"	20.00- 22.50	2.00- 3.00	10.00-12.00	18.00- 20.00
Sugar & Lid	----	2.50- 3.00	----	----
Tumbler, 9 oz.	----	1.50- 2.00	----	----

*white 2.00-3.00
**frosted 8.00-10.00

"DOTS" AND "SHIPS", McKEE GLASS COMPANY

Red IS the rage in both these patterns even though it is the more plentiful color of both patterns. Thus, **the prices listed for these two patterns are for the red color.** Other colors will sell for slightly less due mostly to lack of demand rather than scarcity.

The "dots" occur in red, blue, green and black with black being the least desirable. The "ships" occur in red and black; again, black, though more scarce, is the least collectible.

All the jars in "Ships" come with both white and clear lids. The clear lids seem more plentiful and are less desirable to collectors and generally lower the price of the dish a dollar. However, for purposes of use, the clear lids have the advantage of allowing you to SEE what the dish contains without lifting the lid.

The "Ships" egg beater bowl, 4th Row, 2nd dish, was one of two pieces broken during photographing; unfortunately, THAT was my wife's. So, if you have one . . ..

	"Dots" On Custard	"Ships" "Dots" On White
Bowl, egg beater, w/lip	4.00- 5.00	4.00- 5.00
Butter dish	18.00-20.00	10.00-12.50
Cannister, utility, 48 oz. (tin lid)	18.00-20.00	----
Cannister, utility, 28 oz. (tin lid)	12.00-14.00	----
*Cannister & lid, round, 48 oz.	10.00-12.00	10.00-12.00
Cannister & lid, round, 40 oz.	10.00-12.00	10.00-12.00
Cannister & lid, round, 32 oz.	8.00-10.00	5.00- 6.00
Cannister & lid, round, 16 oz.	6.00- 7.00	4.00- 5.00
Mixing bowl, 9"	8.00-10.00	8.00-10.00
Mixing bowl, 8"	7.00- 8.00	7.00- 8.00
Mixing bowl, 7"	5.00- 6.00	5.00- 6.00
Mixing bowl, 6"	4.00- 5.00	3.00- 4.00
Pitcher, 16 oz.	15.00-17.50	8.00-10.00
Refrigerator dish, 8"x4"	7.50- 8.50	7.00- 8.00
Refrigerator dish, 4"x4"	6.00- 7.00	4.00- 5.00
Shaker, ea.	4.50- 5.50	3.50- 4.50
Tumbler, footed	----	4.00- 5.00

*Cannisters with cyrstal lids, subtract $1.00.

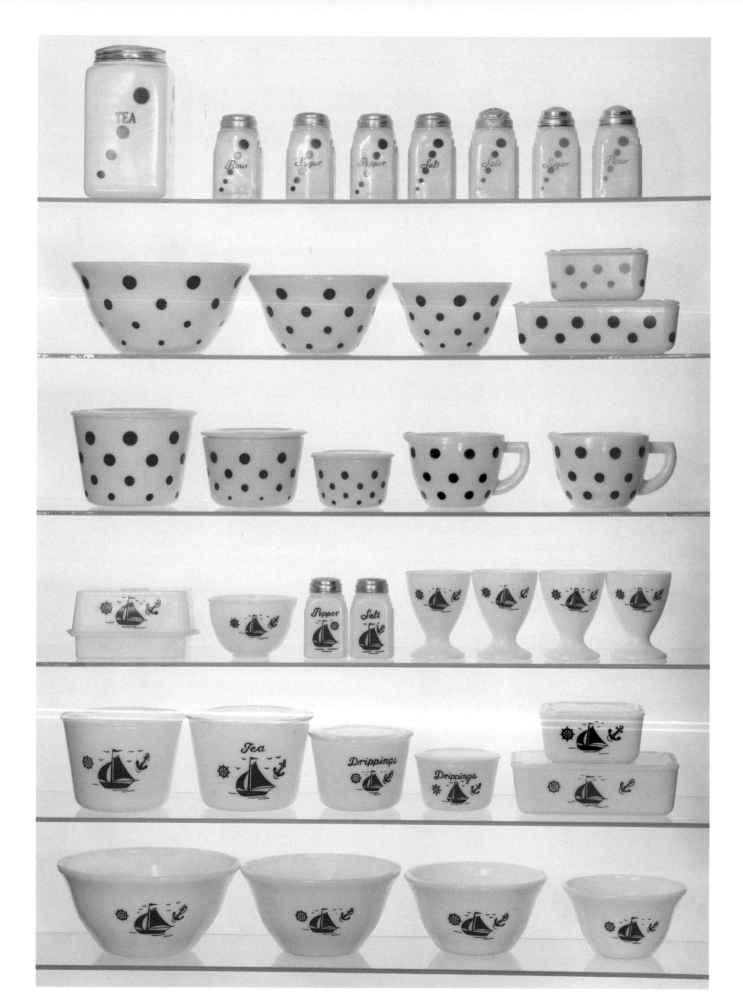

"JENNYWARE", JEANNETTE GLASS COMPANY, 1936-1938

Jeannette's kitchenware items have been commonly called "Jennyware" by collectors for so long that I shan't buck this tradition. Jeannette didn't label it thus. The ultra-marine color is most often found and is the most desired by collectors. Even with few collectors, the crystal reamer is hard to find, as are the pitcher and butter in the ultramarine color. You will notice the ultra-marine butter top pictured had to be "married" to a crystal bottom.

The 16 ounce refrigerator dish doubles as a "grease" jar when combined with the salt and pepper shakers. I strongly recommend you do NOT pour hot grease into this jar, however. You will notice from the picture that the shades of ultra-marine vary, a condition noticeable in the Swirl and Doric & Pansy Dinnerware patterns of Depression Glass. This is due either to being from different runs of glass or from what they call "burn out" of the coloring process, something that happens with glass due to variations of temperature.

	Crystal	Pink	Ultra-marine
Bowl, mixing, 10½"	4.00- 6.00	20.00-22.50	20.00-22.50
Bowl, mixing, 8¼"	2.50- 3.50	6.00- 8.00	7.00- 9.00
Bowl, mixing, 6"	1.50- 2.00	8.00-10.00	10.00-12.00
Butter dish & lid	8.00-10.00	22.00-25.00	30.00-35.00
Measuring cup set	7.00- 8.00	20.00-25.00	20.00-25.00
Measuring, 1 cup	1.50- 2.00	6.00- 7.50	6.00- 7.50
Measuring, ½ cup	1.00- 1.50	5.00- 6.00	5.00- 6.00
Measuring, 1/3 cup	1.00- 1.50	3.00- 4.00	3.00- 4.00
Measuring, ¼ cup	.75- 1.00	2.00- 3.00	2.00- 3.00
Pitcher, 36 oz.	8.00-10.00	30.00-35.00	50.00-60.00
Reamer	45.00-55.00	40.00-47.50	40.00-50.00
Refrigerator dish & lid, 70 oz., round	5.00- 6.00	20.00-22.50	20.00-22.50
Refrigerator dish & lid, 32 oz., round	3.00- 4.00	6.00- 8.00	8.00-10.00
Refrigerator dish & lid, 16 oz., round	2.00- 3.00	8.00-10.00	10.00-12.00
Refrigerator dish & lid, 9"x4½"	3.00- 4.00	10.00-12.00	10.00-12.00
Refrigerator dish & lid, 4½"x4½"	2.00- 2.50	4.00- 5.00	4.00- 5.00
Shaker, ea.	3.00- 3.50	9.00-10.00	9.00-10.00
Tumbler, 8 oz.	3.00- 4.00	10.00-12.00	12.00-15.00

FIRE-KING, ANCHOR HOCKING GLASS COMPANY, blue · 1940's; crystal, ivory and jad-ite

The inclusion of "Fire-King" in my 4th edition *Collector's Encyclopedia of Depression Glass* has started many collector's searching for this very popular ovenware of the early 40's. It was originally guaranteed for two years against breakage, a definite "plus" for that time. Price changes are already being reflected in items now found in short supply or in those items that are very popular such as the 10 3/8" roaster. Collector's have also told me that the nursing bottles are hard to find, particularly the 4 oz. size. I suspect these didn't out last the various "new" generations as well as the cooking items.

The catalogue reprint on the following page is compliments of the Anchor Hocking Glass Company's 1942 four page catalogue, reduced here to one page size. You will notice the glass sold for mere pennies then.

Bakers are the company's term for dishes without lids; lidded dishes are called casseroles.

The prices listed are for Sapphire blue. Crystal, ivory and jad-ite colors will bring about half the prices commanded by blue as they are not as desirable to collectors at this time.

The dripolator shown in row 4, page 15, is Silex. The glass center insert is hard to find undamaged. This dripolator sells for $6.00-8.00.

	Blue		Blue
Baker, 1 pt., round or square	2.00- 2.50	Custard cup, 5 oz.	1.00- 2.00
Baker, 1 qt.	3.00- 4.00	Custard cup, 6 oz, shallow	1.00- 2.00
Baker, 1½ qt.	3.00- 4.00	Custard cup, deep	1.00- 2.00
Baker, 2 qt.	4.00- 5.00	Loaf pan, 9 1/8", deep	5.00- 7.00
Bowl, 2 spout, mixing	6.00- 8.00	Nurser, 4 oz.	5.00- 6.00
Cake pan (deep), 8¾", (roaster)	8.00-10.00	Nurser, 8 oz.	6.00- 8.00
Casserole, 1 pt., knob handle cover	4.00- 4.50	Pie plate, 5 3/8", deep dish	3.00- 4.00
		Pie plate, 8 3/8"	3.00- 4.00
Casserole, 1 qt., knob handle cover	5.00- 6.00	Pie plate, 9"	4.00- 5.00
		Pie plate, 9 5/8"	4.00- 5.00
Casserole, 1½ qt., knob handle cover	6.00- 7.00	Pie plate, 10 3/8" with juice saver rim	10.00-12.00
Casserole, 2 qt., knob handle cover	9.00-10.00	Perculator top, 2 1/8"	2.00- 3.00
Casserole, 1 qt., pie plate cover	6.00- 7.00	Refrigerator jar & cover, 5 1/8"x9 1/8"	8.00-10.00
Casserole, 1½ qt., pie plate cover	9.00-10.00	Refrigerator jar & cover, 4½"x5"	3.00- 4.00
Casserole, 2 qt., pie plate cover	10.00-12.50	Roaster, 10 3/8"	18.00-20.00
Casserole, 10 oz., tab handle cover	6.00- 7.00	Table server, tab handles (hot plate)	6.00- 8.00
Coffee mug, 7 oz., 2 styles	10.00-12.00	Utility pan, 10½", rectangular	5.00- 6.00
Cup, 8 oz. measuring, 1 spout	4.00- 5.00	Utility pan, 8 1/8"x12½"	6.00- 8.00
Cup, 8 oz. measuring, 3 spout	6.00- 8.00		

FIRE · KING OVEN GLASS

Housewives prefer to cook in glass for they are then able to actually see their foods cooking, eliminating the possibility of improperly cooked foods. Glass is also more easily cleaned than metal utensils, saving time and labor.

A three-fold purpose—bake, serve, and store in the same dish. Fire-King oven glass is not only suitable for oven cooking but makes ideal serving dishes for the table and in addition is safe and practical for refrigerator use.

Not only does Fire-King possess unusual cooking qualities but it is attractive, a complement to any table, and above all—the lowest priced oven glass on the market.

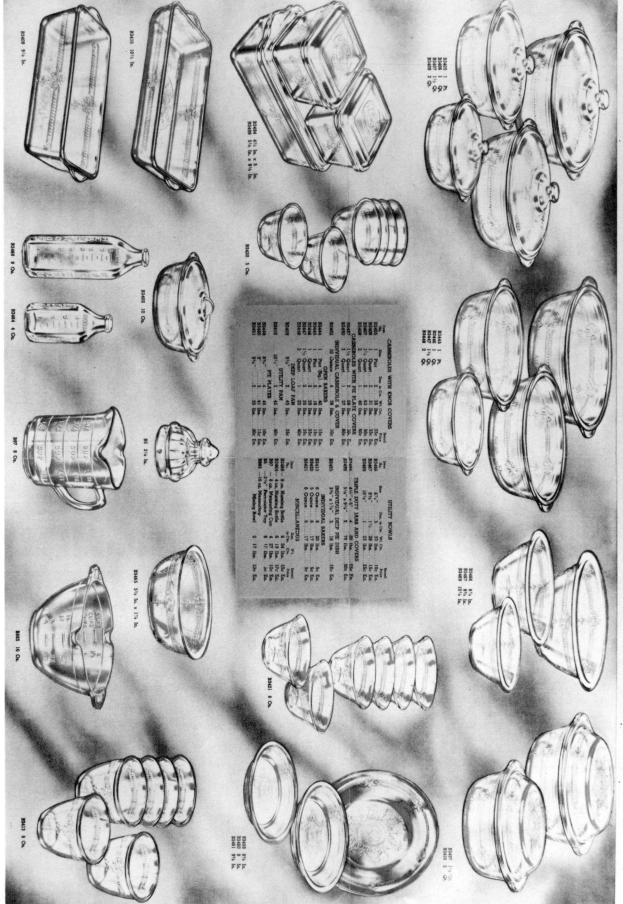

BUTTER DISHES

You will notice that the size and shape of butter has changed over the years. The butter containers here range from ¼ pound to the large 2 pound butter box by Jeannette shown in pink in the last row.

For those who missed the excitement of the French Revolution, someone devised the "guillotine" butter or cheese dish at the top for ease of slicing.

At the end of the fourth row are two ¼ pound butter dishes which are reputed to be the first such dishes ever made. They were manufactured in Pennsylvania and furnished to me by a collector in North Carolina who thought them interesting enough to share.

Notice the picture inset of the metal butter cover on the dish in Row 6.

Row 1: 1st, Embossed "Islay", amber	35.00-40.00
2nd, pink tub	8.00-10.00
green	7.00- 9.00
3rd, white, butter or cheese, w/slicer	45.00-50.00
4th, amber tub	8.00-10.00
crystal	3.00- 4.00
5th, green, ribbed	12.00-15.00
crystal	3.00- 5.00
Row 2: 1st, Skokie green, McKee	12.50-15.00
white	8.00-10.00
2nd, custard, McKee	18.00-20.00
Chalaine blue	30.00-35.00
Seville yellow	27.50-32.50
3rd, crystal, embossed "Butter"	12.00-15.00
Row 3: 1st, custard w/green trim, McKee	10.00-12.00
2nd, "Ships", McKee	10.00-12.50
3rd, white w/flower decal, McKee	12.00-15.00
Row 4: 1st, pink, Federal	15.00-18.00
amber	7.50- 9.00
crystal	3.00- 5.00
2nd, amber, Federal	10.00-12.00
3rd, yellow, Federal	12.00-15.00
4th, green	20.00-25.00
pink	30.00-35.00
crystal	15.00-20.00
Row 5: 1st, white w/red, Hazel Atlas, "Fairmont's"	12.00-15.00
2nd, frosted green, "Crisscross", Hazel Atlas, ¼ lb.	8.00-10.00
3rd, blue, "Crisscross", Hazel Atlas, 1 lb.	30.00-32.50
4th, white w/red, Hazel Atlas, "Fairmont's", round	15.00-17.50
Row 6: 1st, Delphite, Jeannette	35.00-40.00
2nd, pink, "Jennyware", Jeannette	22.00-25.00
3rd, pink, butter box, Jeannette, 2 lb., embossed "B"	35.00-40.00
4th, green, Jeannette bottom, metal cover	10.00-12.00

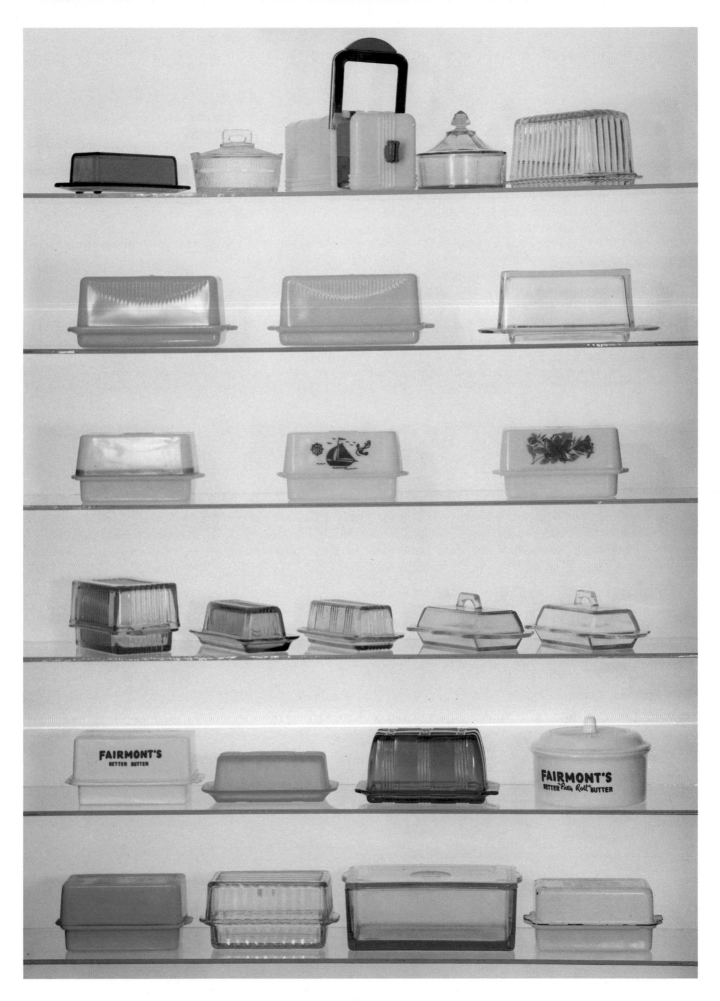

CANNISTER SETS, HOCKING GLASS COMPANY

In the twenties and thirties, if you purchased a golden oak kitchen cabinet with a tilt out flour bin for $30.95 or so (see catalogue reprint section at back of book, page 120), behind the roll curtain door you got a free cannister set so that there would be a "place for everything and everything in its place". These cabinets were extremely popular and helped create a market for cannister sets. Even if you didn't have a cabinet, you wanted cannisters.

All cannisters shown on this page were made by Hocking Glass Company and all are now sought by collectors. In the catalogue reprint section at the back of the book (page 104 and 105), you will notice that the company touted the transparent green cannisters as their "best" or "proven" sellers. This claim would probably hold up today since my wife was buying them long before I deigned to notice "kitchenware". We use the large gallon "cookie" cannisters for flour, sugar, and corn meal. They're a perfect 5 pound size and their air tight lids tend to thwart the efforts of "critters" which like to inhabit grain products.

Least desired are the fired-on colors with black being less happily discovered than red. The condition of the original label on the jars **will** affect the price. On cannisters with glass lids, some roughness will be tolerated on the lids; but chips, nicks and chunks adversely affect the price of the jar. Salt, pepper, sugar and flour shakers have holes in the lids; other spice container lids do not.

Those green provision jars on the third row represent only three of four sizes possible. The ½ pint in this is as elusive as its blue Mason counterpart.

Of the smooth sided cannisters, the choice set to possess is the yellow tinted opaque color rather than the green, red or blue.

Rows 1 & 2:	Green	*Fired-on	Vitrock	Clambroth White	Clambroth Green
Hocking, panelled cannisters					
Cannister, gallon, screw lid	18.00-20.00	----	----	----	----
Cannister, 40 oz., screw lid	12.00-15.00	----	10.00-12.00	----	----
Cannister, 50 oz., glass lid	15.00-17.50	10.00-12.00	----	18.00-20.00	20.00-25.00
Cannister, 20 oz., screw lid	10.00-12.00	6.00- 8.00	6.00- 8.00	----	----
Shaker, ea., rectangular, 8 oz.	5.00- 6.00	2.00- 2.50	4.00- 5.00	5.00- 6.00	8.00-10.00
Shaker, ea., round	5.00- 6.00	----	----	----	----

*Black (flashed on) - 50% less

Rows 3 & 4: Hocking, smooth surface	Fired-on Red	Other Fired-on	Opaque Yellow
Cannister, 40 oz.	12.00-14.00	10.00-12.00	18.00-20.00
Cannister, 20 oz.	6.00- 7.00	5.00- 6.00	12.00-15.00
Shaker, ea., 8 oz.	4.00- 5.00	3.00- 4.00	4.00- 5.00

	Green
Provision jar, ½ pt.	4.00- 6.00
Provision jar, 1 pt.	6.00- 8.00
Provision jar, 1 qt.	8.00-10.00
Provision jar, 2 qt.	10.00-12.00

CANNISTER SETS (and SALT BOXES), JEANNETTE GLASS COMPANY

The blue colored pieces shown in this picture (Jeannette's "Delphite") represent THE most prized color to own of all the Depression era kitchenware. Jeannette's more plentiful green Jadite drops to third place behind Hocking's transparent green panelled items. Many more items than cannisters are available in all three of these colors.

Notice there are two shades of Jadite; there is no price differential between the dark and lighter Jadite at present, at least as far as cannisters are concerned; (darker Jadite reamers command a higher price). You will need to specify light or dark Jadite when ordering through the mail or via phone from a dealer in Depression ware, however.

In the glass lidded cannisters, the lids are the most important piece. You will locate several cannisters sans lids before finding one intact.

Items Available	Delphite	Jadite
Bowl, 4¾" round, ribbed drippings label	20.00-22.50	8.00-10.00
Bowl, 4¾" round, ribbed, no label	15.00-17.50	6.00- 7.50
Cannister, round, ribbed, 40 oz.	20.00-22.50	17.50-20.00
Cannister, round, ribbed, 16 oz.	18.00-20.00	10.00-12.50
Cannister, square, 3" spice w/lid	----	8.00-10.00
Cannister, square, 29 oz., 5" w/lid	25.00-27.50	10.00-12.00
Cannister, square, 48 oz., "Floral" lid	----	12.50-14.00
Shaker, round, ribbed, paper label, ea.		4.00- 5.00
Shaker, round, aluminum top	5.00- 6.00	4.00- 5.00
Shaker, square, ea.	10.00-12.50	3.00- 4.00

Row 4: SALT BOXES, Jeannette

1st box, white	50.00-60.00
crystal	30.00-35.00
2nd box, Jadite	60.00-65.00
3rd box, crystal w/lid	3.00- 4.00
4th box, pink ("Salt" embossed across top)	30.00-35.00
5th box, fired-on red (Owens Illinois?)	5.00- 6.00
crystal	2.00- 3.00

CANNISTER SETS, McKEE GLASS COMPANY

The variety of colors and designs of McKee cannisters is well represented by this picture; however, the "Ships" design cannisters arrived after this picture was made and can be seen in the miscellaneous section of the book (page 67).

McKee called their green "Skokie" green; and like Jeannette's Jadite, the colors of green vary from dark to light. McKee's "Delphite" blue is represented by the 'coffee' cannister in Row 4. The very rare and highly prized "Chalaine" blue is shown in the 'pepper' shaker on Row 2.

In Row 3 we turned one of the decaled cannisters sideways to show the triple Roman arch design typical of many of their cannisters and shakers. The pricing is for the cannisters with decals. Those without decals would sell for less.

The most unusual item shown is the "soap powder" shaker in Row 2. This was not a general catalogue item which leads to the speculation that it may have been a special order item for some sales promotion.

Items Available	Chalaine Blue	Custard	Dots	Seville Yellow	Skokie Green
*Cannister, utility, 48 oz.	22.00-25.00	12.00-14.00	18.00-20.00	18.00-20.00	13.00-15.00
Cannister, utility, 28 oz.	18.00-20.00	8.00-10.00	12.00-14.00	15.00-17.50	8.00-10.00
Cannister & lid, round, 48 oz.	----	8.00-10.00	10.00-12.00	18.00-20.00	10.00-12.00
Cannister & lid, round, 32 oz.	----	7.00- 8.00	8.00-10.00	15.00-17.50	8.00-10.00
Cannister & lid, round, 16 oz.	----	6.00- 7.00	6.00- 7.00	12.00-15.00	7.00- 8.00
*Shaker, panel side, ea.	----	2.50- 4.00	4.00- 5.00	----	3.00- 4.50
**Shaker, square, ea.	12.00-15.00	3.00- 4.00	----	6.00- 8.00	5.00- 6.00

*Delphite Blue, $10.00-12.00
**Soap Powder, $10.00-12.00

	Opal White	Opal White W/Decals	Black
Row 3: Cannister, panel sides, w/decal	8.00-10.00	12.50-15.00	----
Shaker, panel sides, ea.	2.00- 2.50	3.00- 4.00	4.00- 5.00

	Delphite Blue	Seville Yellow
Row 4: Cannister, round, 64 oz.	----	20.00-22.50
Cannister, round, 48 oz.	25.00-27.50	18.00-20.00
Cannister, round, 32 oz.	20.00-22.50	15.00-17.50
Cannister, round, 16 oz.	15.00-17.50	12.00-15.00

CANNISTERS, MISCELLANEOUS

The cannisters pictured here range from choice to "Who cares?". The cobalt blue Hazel Atlas set in the last row is a fine collectible. The 3rd row frosted crystal set is scarcely collectible. Indeed, it upset me to be purchasing them for the book!

There is little demand per se for black cannisters; but there are a number of collectors of black amethyst glass. Therefore, the L.E. Smith black cannisters in Row 1 would soon be snatched up by collectors.

Row 1: 1st cannister, cookie jar, L.E. Smith, black amethyst   22.50-25.00
           2nd cannister, cookie jar, L.E. Smith, black amethyst   18.00-20.00
           3rd cannister, pretzel jar, Anchor Hocking, pink   20.00-22.50
           (See reprint at bottom of page) green   15.00-17.50
           4th cannister, gallon, Owens-Illinois, forest green   10.00-12.00

Row 2: All cannisters, Owens-Illinois, (ovoid shape)

	Crystal	Fired-on Red	Forest Green
Large	8.00- 9.00	9.00-11.00	10.00-12.00
Medium	5.00- 7.00	7.00- 9.00	8.00-10.00
Small (Shaker)	3.00- 4.00	3.00- 4.00	4.00- 5.00

Row 3: All cannisters, Owens-Illinois, squared, diagonal ridge & waffle squares designs

	Crystal (Frosted)	Forest Green
Cannister, 40 oz.	6.00- 7.00	8.00-10.00
Cannister, 16 oz.	4.00- 5.00	6.00- 8.00
Shaker, 8 oz.	1.50- 2.50	2.00- 3.00

Row 4: 1st Cannister, 40 oz., peacock blue   28.00-30.00
           1st Cannister, 40 oz., crystal   8.00-10.00
           2nd Cannister, 16 oz., peacock blue   18.00-20.00
           2nd Cannister, 16 oz., crystal   2.00- 3.00
           3rd - 6th Cannisters, Hazel Atlas, cobalt blue, ea.   30.00-35.00

8-PC. BEER SETS
GREEN GLASS . . . OPTIC PATTERN

80 oz. jug, six 12 oz. handled mugs, 10 in. covered pretzel or cookie jar, pressed green glass.
50R-2075—1 set in carton, 12 lbs......**Set .95**

25

CANNISTERS, UNKNOWN

Many of the cannisters shown here from unknown origins were sold as a part of the deal when you bought a new kitchen cabinet. The bottom row, especially, were the type common to the old "Sellers" cabinets which were so popular in the Depression era.

Remember that many of the shaker sized cannisters were spice cannisters; so, if the label is gone, noticing whether the top has holes or not will be your only clue as to whether you have a spice container or a shaker. Most sets had **four** shakers: salt, pepper, sugar and flour.

The word "tea" was highlighted on the cannister in the second row so the word would show up in the picture.

	Crystal	Green
Row 1: 1st - 4th items		
Cookie jar, 'zipper' panels	10.00-12.00	20.00-22.00
Cannister, 40 oz.	8.00-10.00	12.00-15.00
Shaker or Spice, ea.	1.50- 2.00	5.00- 6.00
5th item: cookie jar, fired-on yellow 5.00- 7.50		

	Clambroth	Crystal
Row 2: Clambroth items:		
Cannisters, large ea. end	20.00-22.50	8.00-10.00
Cannisters, medium, screw lid	12.00-14.00	6.00- 8.00
Cannisters, glass lid	15.00-17.50	----
Shaker or spice	5.00- 7.00	2.00- 2.50
Square cannister, flour label	20.00-22.50	----

Row 3: 1st Cannister, amber 12.00-15.00

	Black Amethyst	Crystal
2nd Cannister, cookie	20.00-22.50	10.00-12.50
3rd Shaker	7.50- 9.00	2.00- 2.50
4th & 5th, Sugar & salt, flashed on green, ea. 7.50- 8.00		

Row 4:
1st Cannister	8.00-10.00
2nd Cannister	5.00- 7.00
3rd Cannister	5.00- 7.00
4th Cannister	8.00-10.00
5th, 6th, 7th Shaker	2.00- 3.00
Spice w/open-close top	4.00- 5.00
8th, Sugar, gallon container	12.00-15.00

DISPENSERS

Technically, these type dispensers were drug store or soda fountain items; however, kitchenware collectors are using these to decorate their kitchens. The "Mission" juice dispensers (each end of 2nd Row) are the most popular with collectors at the moment; with that supply dwindling, the Nesbitt dispensers are catching up as collectibles.

The pink footed bowl on the bottom row is marked "Sunkist" and is very popular with reamer collectors, advertising collectors and kitchenware collectors.

Row 1: Nesbitt's Grapefruit Dispenser, clamp type   35.00- 40.00

Row 2: 1st, Mission juice dispsenser, pink   75.00- 80.00
      3rd, Mission juice dispenser, green   75.00- 80.00
      2nd, Lash's dispenser top (black base and lid
           missing), complete   60.00- 70.00

Row 3: 1st, "Property of Nesbitt's, 'For our syrups only' "   40.00- 50.00
      2nd, "Sunkist" fruit bowl   150.00-175.00

GLASS LADLES AND KNIVES

Glass ladles were made by many different companies, mainly as a part of a mayonnaise set. At the moment, there are only a few serious collectors of these; however, since some of the more unusual colors are commanding "serious" prices, I decided to include them here.

The following is an approximate guide for colors:

amethyst (violet)	8.00-10.00
amber (light or dark)	6.00- 8.00
black	10.00-12.00
*cobalt blue	12.00-15.00
crystal	1.50- 2.50
green	4.00- 5.00
milk white	6.00- 8.00
milk white punch ladle	12.00-15.00
pink	5.00- 6.00
*purple slag	15.00-18.00
yellow	8.00-10.00

*not pictured

Knife drawings courtesy of Margaret Whitmyer.

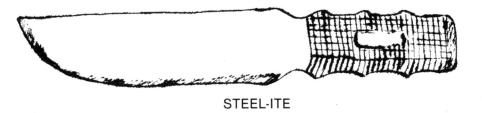

STEEL-ITE

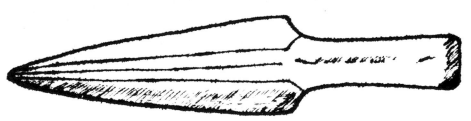

DAGGER TYPE

ROSE SPRAY TYPE

	Crystal	Green	Pink
Knives drawn on this page			
1st knife steel-ite	15.00-18.00	18.00-20.00	22.50-25.00
2nd Dagger type	15.00-20.00	----	----
3rd knife rose spray type	5.00- 6.00	8.00-10.00	8.00-10.00

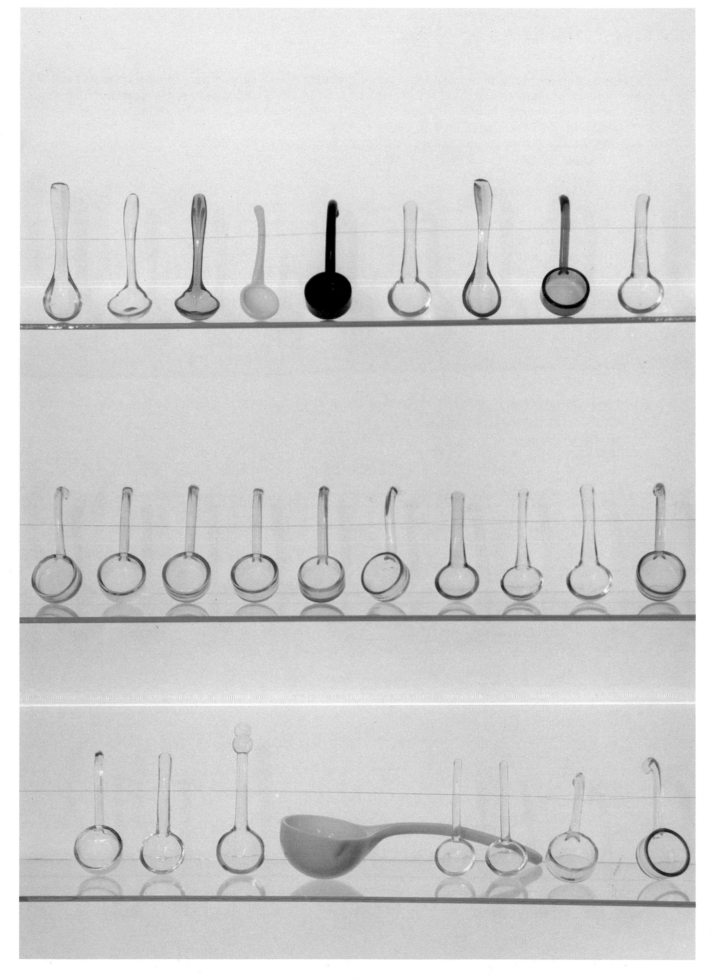

KNIVES (GLASS)

There are increasing numbers of collectors for these glass knives today. These were a very functional item though they look too decorative to be useful. They were made for slicing tomatoes, oranges, lemons and other acid containing fruits and vegetables so that madam housewife didn't discolor her metal knives. In fact, an enclosure with the Dur-X Glass Fruit and Cake Knife states, "I am made of glass, and will not stain or discolor; therefore I am clean, stainless, sanitary and odorless; . . . especially constructed for separating the meaty parts of grapefruit from its rind without punching a hole in the rind."

If the knives dulled, for 25¢ they could be shipped back to the manufacturer to be re-sharpened.

Many of these knives will be found in the original box. Pamphlets enclosed in the boxes advised the user that this box would be the best place to keep the knife. Having an original box will add a dollar to the prices listed below.

Collectors of "Block Optic" Depression Glass Dinnerware pattern often like to buy the block design knife lying on its side in the top row to "go with" their set.

Margaret and I are indebted to Michel Rosewitz for furnishing much of the information and names for these knives.

		Crystal	Green	Pink
Row 1:	1st knife, Pinwheel, 8½"	2.50- 3.00	----	----
	2nd, Quikut handy, 7½"	4.00- 5.00	10.00-12.00	13.00-15.00
	3rd, PAT 12-14-'20 ESP, 9¼"	----	12.00-15.00	----
	4th, Westmoreland Thumbguard, 9¼"	8.00-10.00	----	----
	5th, J.C.W., 9"	6.00- 8.00	----	----
	6th, no mark, unusual, 8¼"	8.00-10.00	----	----
	7, 8 & 9th (lying down), block, 8¼"	4.00- 5.00	10.00-12.00	12.00-15.00

		Blue	Crystal	Green	Pink
Row 2:	1st & 2nd, 5 Leaf Dur-X, 9¼"	10.00-12.00	3.50- 5.00	7.50- 8.50	8.00-10.00
	3rd & 5th, 3 Leaf Dur-X, 8½"	10.00-12.00	3.50- 5.00	7.50- 8.50	8.00-10.00
	4th, 3 Leaf Dur-X, 9¼"	----	3.50- 5.00	----	8.00-10.00
	6th & 7th, 3 Star, 9¼"	10.00-12.00	3.50- 5.00	----	----
	8th, 3 Star, 8½"	10.00-12.00	3.50- 5.00	----	----

		Amber	Crystal	Green	Lt. Amber
Row 3:	1st knife, Westmoreland, 9¼"	----	18.00-20.00	----	----
	2nd B.K. Co. 12-14-'20 Lemons, 9¼"	----	8.00-10.00	----	----
	3rd B.K. Co., 12-14-'20 Flowers, 9¼"	----	7.00- 9.00	----	----
	4th, plain handle, 8¼"	----	----	5.00- 7.50	----
	5th, crystal (odd), 8½"	----	22.00-25.00	----	----
	*6th,				
	7th - 9th (lying down) Stonex, 8¼"	20.00-25.00	----	12.00-15.00	20.00-25.00

*6th is opalescent white but appears brown in the camera lights $45.00-50.00

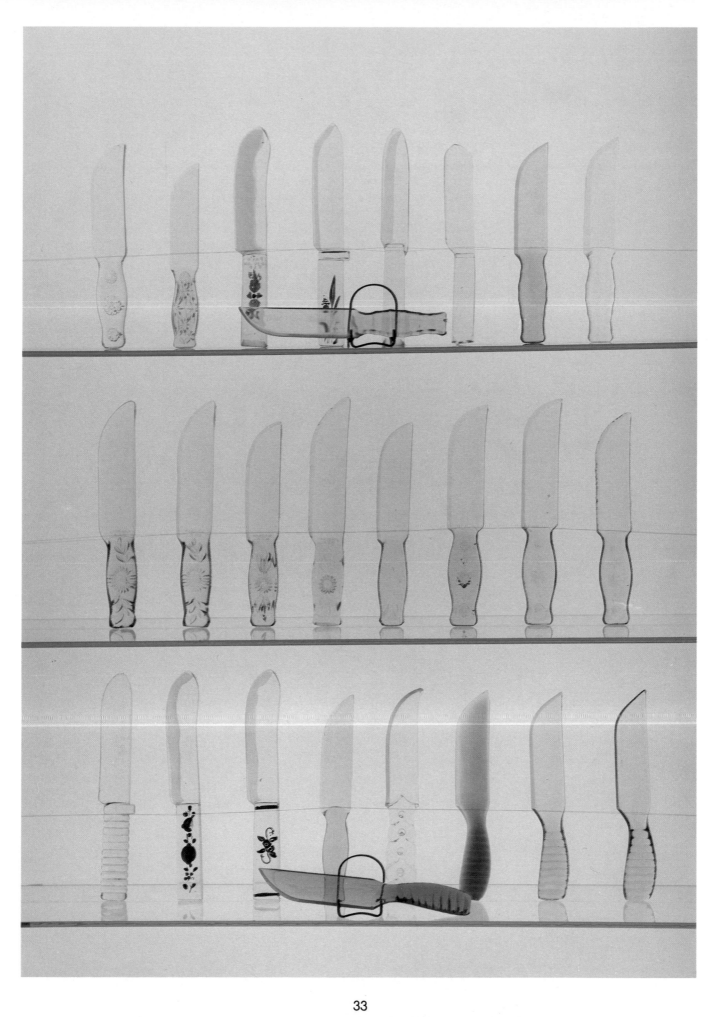

MEASURING CUPS AND PITCHERS

There are few kitchenware items used more than the measuring items pictured which range in size from ¼ cup to 2 cups. Many of the 2 cup variety take reamer tops but are used independently of the reamers more often than not.

In the 5th Row is a two cup, two spouted bowl in Fire-King which I can vouch for being a very handy kitchen item and very collectible, I might add.

The two or three spouted cups are easier to use, but they are also more easily damaged in washing or storing. Three spouts seem to hold more allure for collectors. Too, the amber colored measuring cups are quietly disappearing from the market in the past months.

In Row 4 are Hocking Glass pitchers while in Row 5 are Hazel Atlas pitchers. The Hazel Atlas ones say "Measuring and Mixing Cup" in the bottom whereas the Hocking pitchers are plain.

MEASURING CUPS
CO-734 — 2 doz in carton, 18 lbs **Doz 78c**
8 oz., 3⅝ in., pressed cup and ounce graduated.

Row 1:
1st, "Dots", 2 qt. (rare in black)	15.00-17.50
2nd, Seville yellow, 2 qt.	12.00-15.00
3rd, "Ships", 2 qt.	8.00-10.00
4th, 2 spout, flower design, Skokie green	20.00-25.00
5th, 2 spout, no design, Seville yellow	25.00-30.00

Row 2: Jeannette Glass Co.

	Delphite	Green	Jadite	Pink
1st, 2 cup, Sunflower design in bottom	18.00-20.00	35.00-40.00	12.00-15.00	
2nd, 1 cup, solid handle		6.00- 8.00		12.00-15.00

3rd, 4th, 5th, measuring cups

	Set	Cup	½ Cup	1/3 Cup	¼ Cup
"Jennyware" ultramarine	20.00-25.00	6.00- 7.50	5.00- 6.00	3.00- 4.00	2.00- 3.00
Delphite	25.00-30.00	12.00-15.00	5.00- 6.00	4.00- 5.00	3.00- 4.00
Jadite	12.00-15.00	4.00- 5.00	3.00- 4.00	2.00- 3.00	1.00- 2.00

Row 3:
1st, 3 spout cup, Fry Glass Co.	15.00-18.00
2nd, 1 spout cup, Fry Glass Co.	15.00-18.00
3rd, 1 spout, Federal Glass Co.	10.00-12.00
4th, 3 spout, Federal Glass Co.	12.00-14.00
5th, 3 spout, no handle, Federal Glass Co.	20.00- 25.00
6th, 3 spout	18.00-20.00

Jeannette ACCURATE MEASURING CUPS ½ CUP — USE THEM — IN USE PERFECT RESULTS

Jeannette ACCURATE MEASURING CUPS ½ CUP — USE THEM — TO INSURE PERFECT RESULTS

Row 4: U.S. Glass Co.
1st, 2 cup, pink, etched	15.00-17.50	plain	10.00-12.00
2nd, Handy Andy base			12.00-15.00
3rd, 2 cup, green			10.00-12.00
4th, 2 cup, slick handle, green	10.00-12.00	pink	20.00-25.00
5th, 1 cup, slick handle, 2 spout, green	18.00-20.00	pink	22.00-25.00
6th, 1 cup, no spout, Sellers, green	15.00-18.00	pink	18.00-20.00

Row 5: Hocking Glass Company

	Blue	Crystal	Green	Pink
1st, 2 cup pitcher	75.00-100.00	2.50- 3.00	5.00- 6.00	20.00-22.50
2nd, 2 cup ribbed	----	2.00- 2.50	----	22.50-25.00
3rd, Fire-King, 2 cup, 2 spout	6.00- 8.00	----	----	----
4th, 1 cup, 1 spout	----	----	7.50- 8.50	12.00-15.00

5th, 1 cup, Fire King, 1 spout $4.00-5.00; 3 spout $6.00-8.00.

Row 6: Hazel Atlas Co.

	Blue	Crystal	"Dots"	Green	Pink	White	Yellow
1st - 4th, 2 cup PITCHER only	75.00-85.00	2.00-3.00	12.00-15.00	5.00-6.00	75.00-85.00	3.00- 5.00	150.00-175.00
5th, 1 cup, 1 spout	----	----	----	6.00-8.00	----	----	----
6th, 1 cup, 2 spout	----	2.00-3.00	----	4.00-5.00	----	8.00-10.00	----

MEASURING CUPS AND PITCHERS

In the top row, that seemingly lovely, "Chalaine" blue cries out to be made by McKee, doesn't it? Unfortunately, its twin there in crystal is marked, "Rochester Tumbler Co. Pat. July 13, 1880".

The bowl in Row 5 is also marked "Kellogg's" as are the cups on either side. The last cup in Row 5 says "To be sure of success use Fluffo Shortening and Salad Oil".

First cup in Row 6 tells us to "Use Gillespie's Oriental Flour" and the third cup is marked "Kitchen cabinets - none better - Tippe Canoe".

I mention all these advertisements not just for interest but to clue you to the fact that there are MANY collectors out there who collect advertising items: so, you may find the competition for these kitchenware products to be a bit more fierce than for some of the other wares mentioned in this book.

	Custard	Delphite	Jadite	Seville Yellow
Row 1: 1st & 2nd, McKee, 2 quart	15.00-17.50	35.00-40.00	12.00-15.00	25.00-30.00

Row 1: (cont.) 3rd & 4th, 2 quart, blue $35.00-40.00; crystal $15.00-18.00.

Row 2: Hazel Atlas Glass Co,
1st - 3rd, green (rough finish) $10.00-12.50; white $12.00-15.00; green, $8.00-10.00.
4th, 2 quart, white, green trim, $8.00-10.00.

Row 3: 1st & 2nd, Hocking, 2 quart, green, $8.00-10.00; custard $25.00-30.00.
3rd & 4th, Paden City, 2 quart, green, $25.00-30.00; pink, $29.50-32.50.

Row 4: 1st, U.S. Glass, 'snowflake' in bottom, $14.00-16.00.
2nd, Tufglas, $15.00-20.00.
3rd, U.S. Glass, vaseline, $15.00-18.00.

Row 5: 1st - 3rd, marked "Kellogg's", cups, 3 spout, green, $8.00-10.00; pink, 10.00-12.00.
bowl, $20.00-22.00.
4th, U.S. Glass?, 3 spout, green, $12.00-15.00.
5th, "Fluffo" marked, crystal, $6.00-8.00.

Row 6: 1st cup. "Gillespie's", sun/turned, amethyst $10.00-12.00, crystal $6.00-8.00.
2nd, 1 spout, green, $7.50-8.50.
3rd, "Tippe Canoe", $3.00-4.00.
4th, green, 1 spout, $12.00-15.00.
5th, sun/turned, amethyst $10.00-12.00, crystal $4.00-6.00.
6th, Glasbake, $5.00-6.00; white, $10.00-12.00.

MEASURING CUP

IC778—8 oz., 3 in. high, heavy crystal, well finished, graduated for cups. 4 doz. in carton, 48 lbs..............Doz **48c**

GLASS MEASURING CUPS

No. 3—Half Pint Glass Measuring Cup. Packed 2 dozen to carton.
Per dozen **$1.56**
No. 2—Half Pint Glass Measuring Cup. acked 2 dozen to carton.
Per dozen **$2.20**

36

MECHANICAL ATTACHMENTS

Kitchen gadgets abound and this is only a tip of the iceberg as to what it is possible to collect from that era. You will notice that some of these have motors; but the majority were hand cranked.

Row 1: 1st, beater and jug, $13.00-15.00.
2nd, Wesson Oil Mayonnaise Maker (recipe is embossed in side) $10.00-12.00.
3rd, onion chopper, $6.00-7.50.
4th, beater and bowl, $5.00-6.00.
5th, ruby red beater bowl, $20.00-22.50.

Row 2: 1st, electric beater and bowl, $8.00-10.00.
2nd & 3rd, choppers, $3.00-5.00.
4th, malted milk maker, $6.00-8.00.
5th, egg & cream beater, $10.00-12.00.
6th, electric beater, $5.00-7.00.

Row 3: 1st, electric juicer, Sunkist, $12.00-15.00.
2nd, delphite beater bowl, $15.00-18.00.
3rd, child's glass bake egg beater, $20.00-22.00.
4th & 5th, egg and cream whippers, $3.00-5.00.

Row 4: 1st, ice cube breaker, North Bros. Mfg. Co., $20.00-22.00
2nd, glass sifter, $20.00-22.00.
3rd, reamer, $5.00-6.00.
4th, electric beater, $8.00-10.00.

Mixer shown here $20.00.

Whippers with Bowls

A Complete Outfit—For all light mixing tasks, 2-tone green finish, cadmium plated whipper, 1 pt. graduated glass bowl. On-and-off switch, cord. For A.C. only.

77-3007—1 in box.............Each **1.25**

"POLAR CUB" ELECTRIC FRUIT JUICE EXTRACTOR

1H3190—9½ in. high, 6¾x3½ juice shell, spun aluminum, highly polished, aluminum spout, gray enameled steel body, juice extractor heavily ribbed, designed to extract all juice from fruit, aluminum bottom, rubber tipped to prevent creeping, on and off **toggle switch** cord and attachment plug. 1 in box. Retails $14.50.

Each **$11.50**
6 or more, Each **11.05**

"A & J" EGG BEATER SET

1H5320—Nickel plated steel egg beater, blue tipped white enameled handle, 4¼x4½ glass bowl, graduated from ½ to 2 cups, and ¼ to 1 pt., nickel plated cover. 1 doz. in spaced shipping carton.

Doz **$4.00**

ELECTRIC MIXERS

"**Polar Cub Junior**"—7½x 9½, steel frame, drawn steel motor housing, standard "Universal" motor, base of motor holder and motor gray enameled, other metal parts nickel plated, delft blue finish hardwood handle, toggle switch in head of motor, cord and 2 pc. attachment plug, crystal mixing bowl.

1H3153—1 in box.
Each **$3.75**
3 or more, Each **3.50**

"**Eskimo**"—10½ in., high speed heavy duty motor, **toggle switch**, 5 in. driving rod, 2 types of agitators, heavy cast frame, battleship gray enameled, white enameled handle, rubber feet, cord and plug, 16 oz. glass bowl.

1H3556—1 in box.
Each **$4.95**
3 or more, Each **4.50**

MIXING BOWLS

Individual Depression Era mixing bowls of various sizes are easily found. Complete sets of four to six bowls are more difficult; presently, completed sets are priced more reasonably than buying the same bowls one by one. Bowls are often worn due to use these 40 to 50 years since their issue. Evidence of usage isn't so distressing to collectors of Depression Era KITCHENWARE as to Depression Glass collectors in general as it is practically impossible to find "mint" pieces of kitchenware. See further explanation under the heading "Pricing" at the front of this book.

Row 1: 1st - 3rd bowls, Anchor Hocking; available in 6 sizes and following colors:

	11½"	10¼"	9½"	8½"	7½"	6¾"
crystal	4.00- 5.00	4.00- 4.50	3.50- 4.00	3.00- 3.50	2.00- 2.25	1.00- 1.50
crystal w/trim;						
fired-on	5.00- 6.00	6.00- 7.00	5.00- 6.00	4.00- 5.00	3.00- 4.00	2.00- 3.00
trans. green	8.00-10.00	6.00- 7.00	5.00- 6.00	4.00- 5.00	3.00- 4.00	2.00- 3.00
Vitrock white	8.00-10.00	7.00- 8.00	6.00- 7.00	5.00- 6.00	4.00- 5.00	3.00- 4.00

Row 2: 1st - 4th bowls, Anchor Hocking; available in set of 4 sizes.

	9¾"	8¾"	7¾"	6¾"
crystal	3.00- 4.00	2.00- 2.50	1.50- 2.00	1.00- 1.50
green clambroth	8.00-10.00	7.00- 8.00	6.00- 7.00	5.00- 6.00
green transparent	5.00- 6.00	4.00- 5.00	3.00- 4.00	2.00- 3.00

Fire King blue: see price listing of Fire King on page 12.

Row 3: 1st & 2nd bowls, Federal Glass Co., ribbed with rolled edge (4 sizes).

	10¾"	8¾"	7 7/8"	6 7/8"
amber/green	8.00- 9.00	7.00- 8.00	4.00- 5.00	3.00- 4.00
crystal	4.00- 5.00	3.00- 4.00	3.00- 4.00	2.00- 3.00
pink	10.00-12.00	8.00-10.00	6.00- 8.00	4.00- 6.00

3rd & 4th bowls, Federal Glass Co., ribbed with straight edge (4 sizes).

	9¼"	7½"	6"	5 3/8"
amber/forest green	6.00- 7.00	5.00- 6.00	4.00- 5.00	3.00- 4.00
crystal	4.00- 5.00	3.00- 4.00	2.00- 3.00	1.00- 2.00
fired over white	5.00- 6.00	4.00- 5.00	3.00- 4.00	2.00- 3.00
pink	7.00- 8.00	6.00- 7.00	5.00- 6.00	4.00- 5.00

Row 4: 1st & 2nd bowls, Hazel Atlas Co., ribbed with rolled edge (4 sizes).

	9¾"	8¾"	7¾"	6¾"	
cobalt blue	15.00-18.00	10.00-12.00	8.00-10.00	6.00- 8.00	
crystal	4.00- 5.00	3.00- 4.00	2.00- 3.00	1.00- 2.00	
green/white	7.00- 9.00	6.00- 7.00	5.00- 6.00	3.00- 4.00	
pink	8.00-10.00	7.00- 9.00	6.00- 7.00	5.00- 6.00	

3rd & 4th bowls, Hazel Atlas "REST-WELL" (5 sizes).

	9¾"	8¾"	7¾"	6¾"	5¾"
cobalt blue	25.00-30.00	20.00-22.50	15.00-17.50	12.00-14.00	8.00-10.00
crystal	4.00- 5.00	3.00- 4.00	3.00- 4.00	2.00- 3.00	1.00- 2.00
green/white	8.00-10.00	6.00- 7.00	6.00- 7.00	5.00- 6.00	3.00- 4.00
pink	10.00-12.00	8.00-10.00	7.00- 9.00	6.00- 7.00	5.00- 6.00

Row 5: 1st & 2nd bowls, Hazel Atlas "Crisscross' (4 sizes) priced on page 6.
3rd & 4th bowls, rounded and plain (5 sizes).

	9"	8"	7"	6"	5"
cobalt blue	12.00-14.00	9.00-11.00	8.00- 9.00	7.00- 8.00	6.00- 7.00
crystal	4.00- 5.00	3.00- 4.00	3.00- 4.00	2.00- 3.00	2.00- 3.00
green	7.00- 8.00	6.00- 7.00	5.00- 6.00	5.00- 6.00	3.00- 4.00
white	6.00- 7.00	5.00- 6.00	4.00- 5.00	3.00- 4.00	2.00- 3.00
white w/dutch					
design	12.00-15.00	10.00-12.00	8.00-10.00	6.00- 8.00	5.00- 6.00

Row 6: 1st bowl, Hazel Atlas?, 10½" green, $8.00-10.00.
2nd bowl, Anchor Hocking, 9" green, $6.00-7.00.
3rd bowl, Hazel Atlas (5 sizes):

	9"	8"	7"	6"	5"
white w/red trim	7.00- 8.00	6.00- 7.00	5.00- 6.00	4.00- 5.00	3.00- 4.00

MIXING BOWLS, Con't.

Row 1: 1st bowl, Jeannette Glass Co., (4 sizes):

	9"	8"	7"	6"
Delphite blue	16.00-18.00	13.00-15.00	10.00-12.00	8.00-10.00
Jadite Green	8.00-10.00	7.00- 8.00	6.00- 7.00	6.00- 7.00

2nd bowl, concentric rings with plain bottom (1 size): pink, 7¾" $8.00-10.00.
3rd bowl, concentric rings, ringed bottom (1 size): pink, 8" $8.00-10.00.
4th bowl, "Jennyware" (3 sizes). See "Jennyware" see pricing on page 10.

Row 2: 1st bowl, Jeannette, ribbed (3 sizes):

	9¾"	8½"	7"
Delphite	27.50-30.00	18.00-20.00	12.50-15.00
Jadite	25.00-27.50	10.00-12.00	8.00- 9.00

2nd bowl, Jeannette, Hex Optic, straight edge (4 sizes):

	10"	9"	8¼"	7¼"
green	7.00- 8.00	6.00- 7.00	5.00- 6.00	3.00- 4.00
pink	8.00-10.00	7.00- 8.00	6.00- 7.00	4.00- 5.00

3rd bowl, Jeannette, Hex Optic, ruffled edge (3 sizes):

	10½"	8¼"	6"
green/pink	6.50- 7.50	5.00- 6.00	4.00- 5.00

Row 3: 1st & 2nd bowls, McKee Glass Co., smooth exterior (2 sizes):

	9"	7½"
black	17.00-20.00	12.00-15.00
Seville Yellow	12.00-15.00	10.00-12.00
Skokie green	6.00- 8.00	4.00- 8.00

3rd bowl, McKee, Skokie green, 4½"	3.00- 4.00
4th bowl, McKee, Seville yellow, 3¾"	4.00- 5.00
4th bowl, McKee, white	2.50- 3.50

Row 4: 1st bowl, "Hamilton Beach" Mixer Bowl:

	9¾"	6¾"
opaque yellow	6.00- 7.50	3.00- 5.00
opaque green	3.00- 5.00	2.50- 3.00

2nd bowl, "Magic Maid" mixing bowl:

	10"
green	4.00- 5.00
opal	6.00- 8.00

3rd bowl, tab handled: green, 9¾" 5.00- 6.00

Row 5: 1st bowl, straight sided (not for mixer): green, 9¾"   12.50-14.00
2nd mixing bowl with lip: green, 6½"   2.00- 3.00
3rd bowl, ribbed mixing bowl: custard, 6½"   3.50- 5.00
4th bowl, red & black ringed, 6¼"   1.25- 2.00

Row 6: 1st, 2nd & 3rd bowls, McKee, parts of a four piece set but showing various design possibilities.

	9"	8"	7"	6"
Custard	10.00-12.00	8.00-10.00	7.00-8.00	5.00- 6.00
Skokie green	8.00-10.00	7.00- 8.00	5.00-6.00	4.00- 5.00

4th bowl, McKee, egg beater bowl with lip in "Ships" pattern.
See pricing for "Ships" and "Dots" patterns on page 8.

MIXING BOWLS, Con't.

Row 1: 1st bowl, U.S. Glass Co., 8¾" handled bowl with lid

green	10.00-12.00	14.00-16.00 w/lid	lid only 3.00- 4.00
pink	12.00-15.00	16.00-19.00 w/lid	lid only 3.00- 4.00

2nd bowl, U.S. Glass Co., 9" ribbed, two handled bowl

green	12.00-14.00	same bowl sans ribs	10.00-12.50
pink	14.00-16.00	same bowl sans ribs	12.00-13.50

Row 2: 1st bowl, U.S. Glass Co.

	9"	7"	5"
green	8.00-10.00	6.00- 8.00	4.00- 6.00
pink	10.00-12.00	8.00-10.00	6.00- 8.00

2nd bowl, "Tufglas, 'No Splash Mixer'"   15.00-18.00
3rd bowl, "D & B" embossed on bottom; "Pat appl for" on handle.

green	8.00-10.00
pink	10.00-12.00

Row 3: 1st & 2nd bowls, possibly L.E. Smith; 3 sizes:

8¼"	7¼"	6¼"
18.00-20.00	12.00-15.00	10.00-12.00

3rd bowl, "H.G. Co." embossed on bottom: green, 7½"   3.00- 4.00
4th bowl,   pink, 5¼"   3.00- 4.00

Row 4: 1st bowl, Hocking jadite Fire-King batter bowl   4.00- 5.00
2nd bowl, Federal white batter bowl   3.00- 4.00
3rd bowl, Hazel Atlas crystal batter bowl   2.00- 3.00

Row 5: Anchor Hocking Fire-King blue, 1957 issue:

9½"	8½"	6"	Oval
2.50- 3.00	2.00- 2.50	1.00- 1.50	2.50- 3.50

Row 6: 1st bowl, Anchor Hocking Fire-King, 1950's issue; assorted "Dot" colors.

	9½"	8½"	6"
"Dot", assorted colors	2.00- 3.00	1.50- 2.00	1.00- 1.50

2nd & 3rd bowls, Hocking's Vitrock (6 sizes), priced previously on page 40.

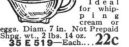

RANGE SETS

These types of sets go by several names, drip sets, grease sets, or range sets. Hocking called them "range sets", so I chose to follow their lead. The Vitrock sets with their various trims shown in the bottom three rows were highly promoted by Hocking through hardware stores with the following sales pitch: "Glassware for kitchen, table and gift use, always attracts women. They are constantly buying new pieces! Glassware seems to be a 'natural' for Hardware Store use as a Traffic Bringer" (See page 117). Well, it evidently worked as these are the most commonly found of all the range sets. Prices are for three piece sets unless otherwise specified.

Row 1: 1st Set, McKee, "Ships"
          "Ships"/large dripping and shakers   13.00-15.00
          "Ships"/small dripping with shakers   11.00-13.00
          2nd Set, Jeannette, "Jennyware", ultra-marine, drip jar & shakers   25.00-30.00

Row 2: 1st Set, Hazel Atlas, white/black, drip w/shakers   20.00-22.00
                             white/green   18.00-20.00
          2nd Set, Horn of Plenty decals, drip w/shakers   10.00-12.00
          3rd, Flour or Sugar Shaker   20.00-25.00

Row 3: 1st Set, "Sailboats" (design on top of drip)   8.00-10.00
          2nd Set, Jeannette, Delphite (drip w/shakers)   30.00-35.00
          3rd Set, Hocking green panelled   20.00-22.00

Row 4: 1st Set, Hocking Vitrock (drip w/shakers)   16.00-18.00
          2nd Set, Anchor Hocking, green, 1950's   6.00- 8.00
          3rd Set, Hocking Vitrock, 3 pc. set, Flower Pot Design   8.00-10.00

Row 5: 1st & 2nd Sets, Hocking Vitrock, 3 pc.   8.00-10.00
          3rd Design - See 2nd Set, Row 6

Row 6: 1st Set, Hocking, opaque yellow   20.00-25.00
          2nd Set, Hocking 5 piece range set, complete   12.00-15.00

REFRIGERATOR CONTAINERS

Row 1: 1st - 5th dishes, Anchor Hocking; oval stacking dishes that have handle indented lids.

	8"x8"	8"x4"	4"x4"	8" Oval	7" Oval	6" Oval
green	6.00- 8.00	4.00- 5.00	2.00- 2.50	6.00- 8.00	4.00- 5.00	2.00- 3.00
Vitrock	10.00-12.00	5.00- 8.00	3.00- 5.00	8.00-10.00	6.00- 8.00	5.00- 6.00

Row 2: 1st & 2nd dishes, Anchor Hocking, no handle indents on top

	8"x8"	4"x4"
trans. green	6.00- 8.00	4.00- 5.00
yellow	15.00-20.00	10.00-15.00

3rd & 4th dishes, rectangular with indent handle (shown in Row 3).

Row 3: 1st dish, Anchor Hocking, indented handles, priced as in Row 1.
2nd dish, Anchor Hocking, indented handles, pk. 4"x4" $10.00-12.00.
3rd dish, "Vegetable Freshener" embossed on top   20.00-25.00

Row 4: 1st bowl, Federal Glass Co., round ribbed, ribbed top;
2nd bowl, Federal Glass Co., ribbed with flat top:

amber	2.00- 3.00
crystal	.50- 1.00
pink	4.00- 5.00

3rd, 4th, 5th dishes, rectangular, ribbed with wide panel corners:

	8"x8"	8"x4"	4"x4"	4"x4" w/'legs'
amber	5.00- 7.00	4.00- 5.00	2.00- 4.00	4.00- 6.00
crystal	1.50- 2.00	1.00- 1.50	.50- 1.00	1.50- 2.00
pink	8.00-10.00	5.00- 7.00	4.00- 5.00	5.00- 7.00

Row 5: 1st, Large crock, jadite, $12.00-14.00.
2nd, 32 oz. round jar & cover, jadite $7.00-8.00, delphite $12.00-15.00.
3rd, Small crock and cover, green, $5.00-6.00.
4th, Jennyware, 16 oz., $10.00-12.00.

Row 6: 1st - 4th, Jeannette's plain, rectangular & square stacking refrigerator dishes.

	4"x8"	4"x4"
Delphite (blue)	10.00-12.50	7.50- 8.50
Jadite (green)	7.00- 8.00	4.00- 5.00
Ultramarine	8.00-10.00	5.00- 6.00

1C1981—4⅝ x 2⅛, plain crystal with 2 handles, cover with sunken lift handle. 3 doz. in carton, 60 lbs.....**Doz 92c**

1C1978—3½x4½, round, clear crystal, sunk handle. 3 doz. in carton, 53 lbs. **Doz 92c**

1C1982—5x4¼x2, oblong shape, good quality crystal, double handled, fitted cover with sunk-in lift. 4 doz. in case, 80 lbs.....**Doz 96c**

1C1889—2 lb., 6x 4¼, clear crystal, sunk handle, plain bottom. 1 doz. in carton, 40 lbs. **Doz $1.89**

6 Piece Emerald Green Glass Kitchen Set

6 sets in barrel, 90 lbs., SET (6 pcs)

72c

Regular retail value $1.40—A wonderful $1.00 window leader.

1C1764—6 PIECES, heavy pressed transparent emerald green glass, well made and finished.

1 each of the following:

FOOD CONTAINER—6¼x4¼, covered.   MIXING BOWL—8¼ in., deep.
BUTTER JAR—5x4½, covered.   MIXING BOWL—7¼ in., deep.
REAMER SET—Graduated 1 qt. pitcher and perforated reamer cover (counts as 2 pcs.).

REFRIGERATOR CONTAINERS

Row 1: 1st dish, Jeannette's green "Floral", pattern.

	4"x8"	4"x4"
Green	----	22.00-25.00
Jadite (pictured in Row 2)	17.50	10.00-12.50

2nd dish, "Jennyware", Jeannette, (see page 10).
3rd & 4th dish, "Hex Optic":

	4"x4"	Round W/Lid	Round Set (3)
green	4.00- 5.00	3.00-4.00 ea.	12.00-15.00
pink	5.00- 7.00	4.00-5.00 ea.	15.00-18.00

Row 2: 1st & 2nd "Floral" dishes by Jeannette: see Row 1, this page, for pricing.
3rd dish, Jeannette, batter pitcher, Jadite.   30.00-35.00

Row 3: 1st & 2nd dishes, Hazel Atlas, "Platonite":

5" round w/foot	2.00- 2.50
6" round	5.00- 7.50

3rd - 5th dishes:

	5¾" Round	5¾" Knob Lid	4½"x5½"
green	3.00- 4.00	3.50- 4.50	2.50- 3.50
pink	6.00- 8.00	----	6.00- 7.50

Row 4: 1st - 4th dishes, Hazel Atlas, "Crisscross" design, (see page 6).

Row 5: 1st dish, "Tufglas", 6½" square   16.00-20.00
2nd dish, McBeth Evans stack set, pink   20.00-25.00
3rd dish, McKee, "Glasbake", 5"   2.50- 3.00
4th dish, unknown maker, 3"x3"   1.00- 1.50

Row 6: 1st dish, crystal, tri-sectioned of unknown origin; lid?   5.00- 8.00
2nd dish, crystal, ribbed with lid   2.50- 3.00
3rd dish, green, double tab handle (knife rest?)   12.50-15.00

Green Glass Ice Box Sets

3 Jars—1 Cover

Pressed green glass, 3 jars, 5¾ in. diam., 2⅜ in. high, raised cover fits each jar, each set in box.

50R-3092—½ doz sets in carton, 36 lbs.

Doz sets 1.95

Icebox Set

Made from pressed glass colored a delicate green. Three compartments, interfitting. Six inches high by 5 by 4½ inches. It takes care so handily of those left overs that you can never find space for in any other way. Weight, packed, 4 lbs.
35N6833..........63c

SANITARY GLASS FOOD CONTAINER

Serves double purpose of food or butter jar and also as mixing bowl.

THIS MONTH ONLY

IC1880—6¼ in. diam., clear crystal, deep shape, sunk-in knob cover. 2 doz. in carton, 50 lbs. **Doz $1.45**

REFRIGERATOR CONTAINERS, Con't.

Row 1: 1st & 4th, Hocking water bottles.

crystal	2.00- 3.00
green	6.00- 8.00

2nd, 3rd, 5th, Owens-Illinois bottles.

crystal	3.00- 5.00
forest green	5.00- 7.00

Row 2: 1st, Ownes-Illinois water bottle.

crystal	2.00- 3.00
forest green	5.00- 7.00

2nd, Hocking water bottle.

crystal	2.00- 3.00
green	6.00- 8.00

3rd & 4th, McKee refrigerator dishes with flanged lids:

	7"	7" Flower Motif	6"	6" Flower Motif
green	14.00-16.00	16.00-18.00	12.00-14.00	14.00-16.00
yellow	20.00-22.00	22.00-25.00	18.00-20.00	20.00-22.00

Row 3: 1st dish, McKee Skokie green covered dish (2 sizes):

	4"x8"	4"x4"
custard	6.00- 7.50	4.00- 5.00
Seville yellow	15.00-17.50	8.00-10.00
Skokie green	6.00- 7.50	4.00- 5.00
white	5.00- 6.00	3.00- 4.00

2nd dish, McKee "Ships". See "Ships" priced on page 8.
3rd dish, McKee Seville yellow tray, 8¼"x12½"   15.00-20.00

Row 4: 1st - 6th dishes, McKee "Dots" and "Ships" refrigerator dishes, priced on page 8.

Row 5: 1st - 3rd dishes, parts of "Hall's" Water Cooler Set (possibly McKee).
Set includes:

Dispenser (water)	35.00- 40.00
4"x6" bowl with lid	8.00- 10.00
Butter Dish	18.00- 20.00
Large Tray (possibly defroster tray, not shown)	10.00- 12.50
Set Complete	75.00- 80.00

Row 6:

1st, crystal water dispenser	10.00- 12.00
2nd, McKee Jadite green dispenser	50.00- 60.00
3rd, L.E. Smith, cobalt blue dispenser	125.00-150.00

ROLLING PINS, BAKING ITEMS, Etc.

I'm told that cold water inside the rolling pins made the dough easier to roll; then again, some-one explained that those "shaker" tops on the end of the older rolling pins made it easier to add sprinklings of flour where needed. Obviously you chose one or the other method. The older glass roll-ing pins are not easily found in colors leading me to wonder if there should be some credence given those tales of the wife bashing her husband's head with the rolling pin.

Most of the ovenware is Glasbake. There appear to have been 5 sizes of the heart shaped "cherry pie" dishes.

Row 1:	Cake tube, Glasbake	4.00-	5.00
	2nd, cake tub, Glasbake	6.00-	8.00
	3rd, casserole, ftd., Glasbake	7.50-	8.00
Row 2:	1st Syrup	15.00-	17.00
	2nd Syrup, "Ball"	4.00-	5.00
	3rd, Toothpick	5.00-	7.00
	4th, Custards, Glasbake	.35-	.50
	5th, Pan w/handle, Glasbake	5.00-	7.00
Rows 3 & 4:	Rolling Pins: (pictured) Crystal tube	5.00-	8.00
	(pictured) White, Imperial	20.00-	25.00
	(pictured) White, unmarked	18.00-	20.00
	(pictured) Jadite	75.00-	85.00
	(pictured) Clambroth	50.00-	55.00
	(not pictured) Amethyst	75.00-	85.00
	(not pictured) Black Amethyst	65.00-	75.00
	(not pictured) Cobalt blue	75.00-	85.00
	(not pictured) Delphite blue	100.00-	115.00
	(pictured page 65) Chalaine blue	110.00-	125.00
Row 5:	1st, egg cup	2.50-	3.00
	2nd, "Apple" shaped pie dish	2.50-	3.50
	3rd, Child's egg beater	20.00-	22.00
	4th - 6th, Child's Glasbake items, ea.	4.00-	5.00
Row 6:	Heart Shaped "Cherry Pie" dishes, 10½", 9½", 8½", 7½", 6½", ea.	2.00-	3.00

35N7826 — Angel Food Tube Cake Pan. Size, 3½x8 in. Weight, packed, 6¾ lbs...**$1.55**

Hollow Glass Rolling Pin
Pressed glass, with cork lined metal cap. Easily filled with cold water, which keeps pie crust cold and prevents dough from sticking to roller. Weight, packed, 3½ pounds.
35N6103..............................**42c**

SHAKERS, SPICE JARS & SYRUPS

I have priced these shaker and spice items individually. When setting up for photographing these, we generally picked one type, color or design to show. However, please be sure that **most of the shaker and spice jars are available in at least a basic set of four items, those being the salt, pepper, flour and sugar**; and some are available in a great variety of labels such as cocoa, nut meats, paprika, etc. If you haven't tried an 8 ounce stove top shaker, you've missed a great bet. I found that out when my wife bought a pair of the Hocking green ones several years ago "because they reminded her of a pair she'd seen on her grandmother's shelf above the stove". Suddenly, you could salt and pepper without shaking your arm off or rushing to refill a shaker it seemed you'd just filled a couple of days before.

The 4th Row shows sugar shakers. Please notice the one with the **glass** top that has managed to survive all these years. I personally dislike the second type because it's a pain to fill. With the advent of the sugar bowl, sugar shakers went out of vogue except at the local truck diner; that's a loss as I've discovered since having one at the house.

Row 1:   1st - 6th Shakers or spice jars, Hocking, panelled, rectangular, 8 oz. ea.

Clambroth Green	Green	Fired-on Red	Fired-on Black	Vitrock
8.00-10.00	5.00- 6.00	2.00- 2.50	2.50- 3.00	4.00- 5.00

7th - 9th, Hocking, smooth surface, rectangular, 8 oz. ea.

Fired-on Red	Other Fired-on Colors	Opaque Yellow
4.00- 5.00	3.00- 4.00	4.00- 5.00

Row 2:   Shakers, Hocking, round
       1st & 2nd, green, ea.   5.00- 6.00
       3rd - 6th, Vitrock/patterns   1.50- 2.50

Row 3:   1st - 5th Shakers, Anchor Hocking, 1950's   1.50- 2.00
       6th - 10th Shakers, Owens-Illinois:

	Fired-on Red	Forest Green
square bottom	----	2.00- 3.00
ovoid bottom	3.00- 4.00	4.00- 5.00

Row 4:   1st Sugar shaker, glass top: green, $40.00-45.00; crystal, $20.00-22.50.

2nd Sugar shaker, pink	35.00-37.50
3rd Sugar shaker, pink	32.00-35.00
4th Sugar Shaker, (w/lid), pink	22.00-25.00
5th Sugar shaker, amber	30.00-35.00
6th Sugar shaker, green	20.00-22.00

       7th & 8th Sugar shakers, green $20.00-22.00; pink, $30.00-35.00
                     Jadite $26.00-30.00

Row 5:   1st Syrup, Cambridge, etched set   35.00-40.00
                          no etching, set   20.00-25.00

2nd Creamer, amber	4.00- 5.00
3rd Syrup, pink	18.00-20.00
4th Syrup, Heisey, yellow	32.00-35.00
5th Syrup, pink	18.00-20.00

Row 6:   1st, Syrup, green   8.00-10.00
       2nd Syrup, McKee, crystal   6.00- 8.00
       3rd Syrup, pink, $25.00-30.00; green   10.00-12.00
       4th & 5th Syrups, green, $10.00-12.00; pink   18.00-20.00
       6th Syrup or batter jug, complete   18.00-20.00

SHAKERS

McKee and Jeannette shakers make up the majority of those shown here. Again, the blue colors are the most desired by collectors---a view with which I heartily concur since blue has ever been my color!

Notice the tray holder for the shakers in the top row. You will often find the spice sets on these handy containers which, depending upon condition, should add a dollar or so to the price. Again, shakers are priced each and are not differentiated from spice jars.

Row 1: Shakers, McKee Glass Co., 8 oz. sq. bottom, ea.

	Black	Chalaine Blue	Custard	Skokie Green
	4.00- 5.00	12.00-15.00	3.00- 4.00	5.00- 6.00

Row 2: Shakers, Roman arch side panel, 6 oz., ea.

	Black	Custard	"Dots"	Skokie Green	White	White W/Design
	3.00- 4.00	2.50- 4.00	4.00- 5.00	3.00- 4.50	2.00- 2.50	2.50- 3.00

Row 3: Shakers, McKee
     "Ships", 6 oz.   4.50- 5.50
     "Soap Powder", Skokie green, unusual marking, 8 oz.   10.00-12.00
     All others priced as in Row 1 and Row 2

Row 4: Shakers, Jeannette Glass Co.

	Crystal	Pink	Ultra-marine
1st & 2nd Shakers, "Jennyware", 8 oz., ea.	3.00- 4.00	9.00-10.00	9.00-10.00
	Delphite	Jadite	
3rd, 4th & 5th 8 oz., square bottom, ea.	10.00-12.50	3.00- 4.00	
6th, 7th Small, round, ea.		4.00- 5.00	
8th-11th Large, round, ea.	5.00- 6.00	4.00- 5.00	

Row 5: 1st, Black amethyst   7.50- 8.50
      2nd, Black amethyst, handled   8.00-10.00
      3rd & 4th, Clambroth   5.00- 7.00
      5th & 6th, Embossed labels, green or blue   15.00-18.00
      7th, White   2.00- 3.00
      8th, White w/decoration   1.00

Row 6: Kitchen Cabinet Shakers
      1st & 2nd, crystal handled, ea.   1.75- 2.50
      3rd - 6th, crystal shakers   1.00- 1.50
           crystal w/open-close top (shown at bottom)   2.00- 2.50
      7th, 'zipper' panels, green   5.00- 6.00
      8th, pink   5.00- 6.00

59

SHAKERS

Generally speaking, the small, square shakers like those along the top row are marked "Tipp City". They're very plentiful in the mid-western area.

Collectors of the "Cattail" China often capture the shakers at the end of the first row for their stove set. They come as a set of four: salt, pepper, sugar and flour.

A number of these shakers were given away as premium items---even the "Dutch" set in the fourth row appears to have been packed with cottage cheese, at least that's what the top of the salt item says. Too, the "Home Soap Company of Pittsburg, Pa." appears to have packaged some product in the 3rd shaker of the third row.

The shaker at the center of the bottom row has the most specific label we've come across, however, "Roastmeat Seasonings".

Row 1: "Rooster" shaker (set w/stand: $6.00)   2.00- 3.00
   "Basket" shaker, Tipp City   1.00- 1.50
   "Scottie" shaker   1.50- 2.00
   "Belle" shaker   1.00- 1.50
   "Cattail"   3.00- 4.00

Row 2: "Dutch Children", (Boxed Set: $6.00-8.00)   1.00- 1.50
   "Cornucopia"   1.00- 1.50
   "Sailboats"   1.00- 1.50
   "Dutch Maiden" Salt ("Dutch Boy", red/white pictured in back) 1.50- 2.00
   Shakers, cobalt   2.50- 4.00

Row 3: Small white   1.00- 1.50
   Large white   2.00- 2.50
   3rd Shaker, "Home Soap Co.", unusual label, advertising   5.00- 8.00

Row 4: "Dutch Design", latice embossed, crystal, 12 oz.   4.00- 5.00
          crystal, 16 oz.   6.00- 7.00

Row 5: Shaker, embossed labels, green   7.50- 8.50
         pink   8.00- 9.00
   "Dutch", fired-on colors (over white) of yellow, red, blue, green 1.50- 2.50
   8th Shaker, white, "Dutch Boy"   2.50- 3.00

Row 6: Dutch Children Spice Set ("Dove" spice label on back) w/rack   12.00-14.00
   individual shakers   1.50- 2.00
   Large white shakers (except "Roastmeat Seasonsings" $4.00-5.00) 2.00- 2.50

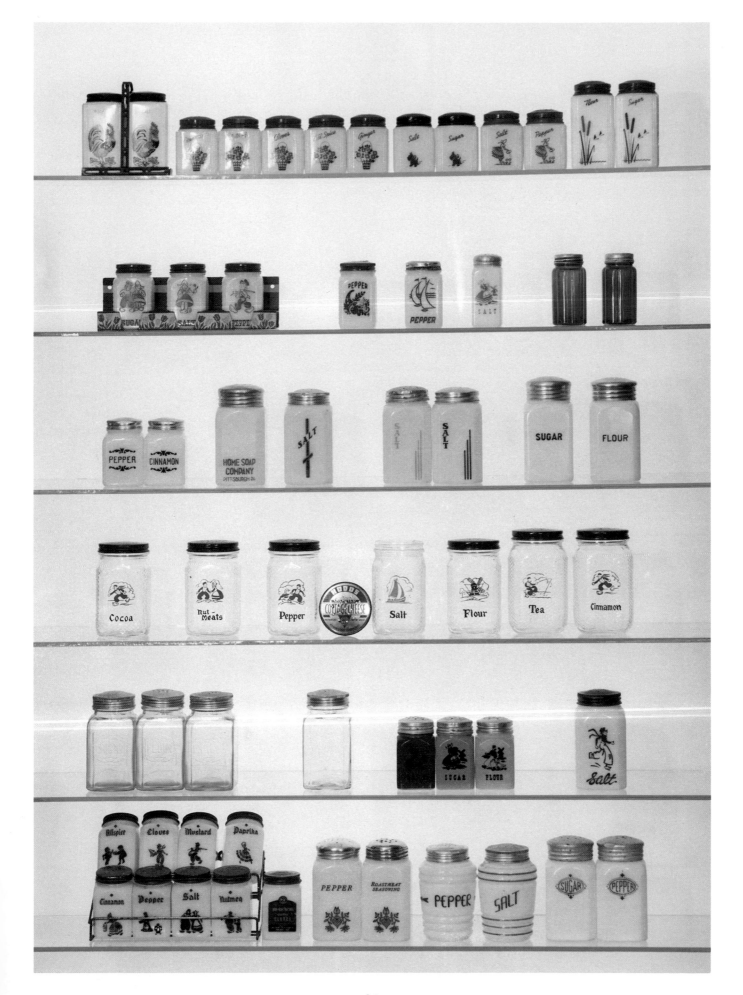

LATE ARRIVALS

There is no rhyme nor reason to the following ten pages---except that these were items that came after the original photography session or were items that the negatives were lost after a devastating fire at the photographer's building.

Noteworthy are the clambroth pickle dipper, Row 1; the black amethyst tray under the bath set, Row 1; the blue Jeannette "matches" dish in Row 2; and the "Sanitary Cheese Preserver" in the last Row. This dish instructs one to "Remove Lid Daily" and to "Place ½ pint vinegar and ½ tablespoon full of salt in bottom slightly dilute with water"; "Pat applied for".

Row 1:	1st, Large funnel, crystal	8.00-10.00
	2nd, Small funnel, crystal $3.00-4.00, pink	12.00-15.00
	3rd, Pickle ladle, clambroth	8.00-10.00
	4th, Bath set and tray, jadite & black amethyst, respectively	25.00-30.00
Row 2:	Bath items, Jeannette (note two shades of jadite), ea.	8.00- 9.00
	2nd, "Miracle Maize" corn stick	5.00- 7.00
	3rd, "Matches" holder, Jeannette, delphite, $12.00-14.00; jadite	7.00- 8.00
	same as above with no label, delphite, $7.00-7.50; jadite	3.00- 3.50
Row 3:	1st, Custard, "Fy/Rock", blue	2.00- 3.00
	2nd & 3rd, Custards, ea.	1.50- 2.00
	4th, Casserole w/metal holder, Fry	10.00-12.00
	5th, Casserole, oval, Fry	6.00- 8.00
	6th, Pie dish, Fry	5.00- 7.00
Row 4:	1st, Rectangular pan, Fry	5.00- 7.00
	2nd & 3rd, Mugs, handled, 16 oz., green or pink	6.00- 8.00
	4th, Mug, part of Hocking "Pretzel" set. See page 24., green/pink	5.00- 7.00
	5th, Tumbler, Hazel Atlas	2.00- 3.00
	6th, Tumbler, McKee, jadite	5.00- 6.00
Row 5:	1st, 2 cup measure, pink	5.00- 7.00
	2nd, "Naxon", 2 cup measure, green	4.00- 6.00
	3rd, Server, round, tab handles, green	2.00- 3.00
	4th, Egg cup, Jeannette	5.00- 7.00
	5th, Ice server, "Frigidaire"	4.00- 5.00
Row 6:	"Sanitary Cheese Preserver"	17.50-20.00
	2nd, Ice bowl, McKee, black amethyst	12.00-14.00
	3rd, Serving bowl w/ladle, black	12.00-15.00

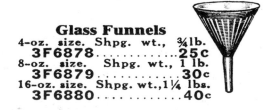

Glass Funnels
4-oz. size. Shpg. wt., ¾ lb.
3F6878 . . . .**25c**
8-oz. size. Shpg. wt., 1 lb.
3F6879 . . . .**30c**
16-oz. size. Shpg. wt.,1¼ lbs.
3F6880 . . . .**40c**

$2¹⁰ 1½ -Qt

Casserole and Holder
Heat quick bottom. Mold etched design. Chrome plated brass frame. With cook book.

Round	Cap. Qts.	Shpg. Wt.	Not Prepaid
9 E 2145	1½	5 lbs. 8 oz.	**$2.10**
Oval **9 E 2146**	2	6 lbs.	2.39

LATE ARRIVALS, Bowls, etc.

The various sizes of these bowls have been priced previously in the book; so only the items shown here will be priced below.

I remember those Fire-King "tulip" bowls. Mom made a lot of good stuff in those when I was little!

The "Chalaine" like color of the rolling pin doesn't show in the picture. The studio lighting turned it an almost brown color; so, we backed it with paper to make it show blue---but it isn't quite the blue it should be.

Row 1: 1st, Fire-King, 9½" "tulip" design bowl, Anchor Hocking   2.00- 2.50
               8½" "tulip" design bowl, Anchor Hocking   1.50- 2.00
               grease container   2.00- 2.50

Row 2: 1st & 3rd, Anchor Hocking, red dot design, 9½"   2.00- 2.50
               6"   1.00- 1.50
   2nd, Rolling pin, "Chalaine" like blue   110.00-125.00

Row 3: 1st bowl, fired-on red   1.00- 2.00
   2nd bowl, ribbed with spout, green: $4.00-5.00; pink   6.00- 8.00
   3rd & 4th, Hazel Atlas Dot design, 5"   2.50- 3.00
               8"   5.00- 6.00

Row 4: 1st, Butter dish, cactus design (McKee?)   15.00- 17.50
   2nd, Refrigerator dish, double tab handle   12.50- 15.00
   3rd, Butter, crystal, L.E. Smith   12.00- 15.00
   4th, Child's egg beater/bowl   20.00- 22.00

Row 5: 1st - 3rd, Hazel Atlas: 4"x4" red dot   5.00- 7.00
               dripping jar   5.00- 7.00
               5¾" refrigerator, round   8.00- 10.00
   4th, Cake preserver, crystal   10.00- 12.00

LATE ARRIVALS, Cannisters & Casseroles

Collectors of the "Taverne" China usually "cabbage" these containers with the Taverne labels. I've seen black and green decals; we have something that appears to be "frosted" Taverne, but I wonder if perhaps the color hasn't just left us over the years.

In the 2nd row is a "Suffragette" or a very militant lady; she's wearing a pan for a hat and carrying a rolling pin like a rifle. The Dutch decal cannisters are from Hocking and need the decals to be worth much.

Fourth row hosts an oval Fry casserole and an unusual frosted vaseline colored Heisey casserole; both come with their own metal holder.

Fifth row shows us a five dish, refrigerator lazy susan storage system.

Row 1: 1st, "Taverne" scene, black, green, possibly "frosted" colors — 10.00-12.50
2nd, Tea cannister, Jeannette, jadite, 16 oz. — 12.50-15.00
3rd, Sugar cannister, Jeannette, jadite, 40 oz. — 17.50-20.00
4th, Coffee cannister, ovoid shape, Owens-Illinois, forest green — 10.00-12.00

Row 2: 1st, "Dots", 16 oz., McKee — 6.00- 7.00
2nd, "Suffragette" embossed cannister, 40 oz. — 10.00-12.50
3rd & 4th, Cannisters w/decals, Hocking — 10.00-12.00
without decals, Hocking — 5.00- 6.00

Row 3: 1st - 3rd, "Ships" cannister, 48 oz., white lids — 10.00-12.00
crystal lids — 9.00-11.00
4th, "Ships" cannister, 40 oz., white lid — 10.00-12.00
crystal lid — 9.00-11.00

Row 4: 1st, Casserole, Fry, etched — 12.00-15.00
2nd, Casserole, Heisey, frosted vaseline — 40.00-45.00

Row 5: 1st, Lazy susan storage set (5 jars) — 12.00-15.00
2nd, Casserole, Fy/Rock blue — 12.00-15.00

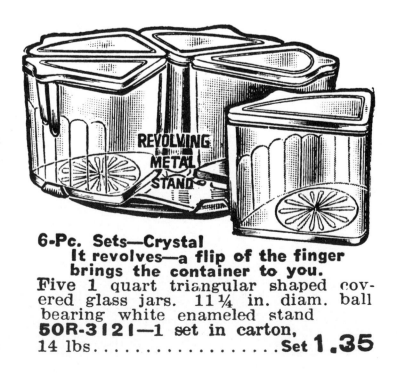

6-Pc. Sets—Crystal
It revolves—a flip of the finger
brings the container to you.
Five 1 quart triangular shaped covered glass jars. 11¼ in. diam. ball bearing white enameled stand
50R-3121—1 set in carton,
14 lbs................**Set 1.35**

66

LATE ARRIVALS, Shakers, Syrups, Cruets

The large set of spice jars shown in the center of the photograph were made by Ball, the canning jar specialists. The large white salt shaker at the beginning of that row is interesting only in that it is embossed "Chef-Boy-Ar-Dee" on the bottom.

Row 1: 1st, Syrup, Heisey   20.00-25.00
          2nd, Cruet, Heisey   22.00-25.00
          3rd, Spice set on "swing" hinged holder, Tipp City   10.00-12.00
          4th, Oil & Vinegar, Heisey pink: $35.00-40.00; crystal   20.00-22.50
          5th, Sugar shaker, Heisey, pink   30.00-35.00

Row 2: 1st Syrup, crystal   10.00-12.00
          2nd Syrup, Heisey   18.00-20.00
          3rd, Cruet, Heisey "Twist", green: $40.00-45.00; pink   30.00-35.00
          4th, Cruet, Heisey, silver overlay   22.50-25.00
          5th, Cruet, Heisey, crystal   20.00-22.50

Row 3: 1st Shaker, "Chef-Boy-Ar-Dee" embossing   4.00- 5.00
          2nd Shaker   2.00- 2.50
          3rd Set, 12 piece Ball spice set w/tray   25.00-30.00
          4th & 5th, Shakers   2.00- 2.50

Row 4: 1st Shaker, "Scottie"   3.50- 4.00
          2nd, Scottie Range Set w/holder   10.00-12.50
          3rd, "Scottie" shaker, ea.   3.50- 4.00
          5th & 6th, Silk hats design   1.50- 2.00

Row 5: 1st - 4th, "Roosters" shakers   2.00- 2.50
          5th, 6th, 7th, Shakers   2.00- 2.50
          8th, Vitrock shaker   4.00- 5.00

MOLASSES CANS

No. 80—Sanitary Plated Top; number dozen in barrel 10; weight 175 pounds; capacity 12 ounces.
Per dozen, barrel price **$6.00**
Per dozen, open stock price . . **6.60**

No. 85—Sanitary Plated Top; number dozen in barrel 5; weight 140 pounds; capacity 28 ounces.
Per dozen, barrel price **$12.00**
Per dozen, open stock price . **13.00**

LATE ARRIVALS, STRAW HOLDERS AND PITCHERS

The disastrous fire that swept through the photography studio destroyed the negatives of the picture that had several more straw holders, so you will forgive us for only showing two of the three sizes known. There is a 10¼" straw holder besides the 9½" and 12" shown.

The U.S. Glass condiment set in the third row remains one of my favorite pieces of kitchenware.

Row 1: 1st*, Owens-Illinois 32 Oz., water bottle (wishing well scene) marked,
        "Pat. Apr. 5, 1932"   4.00- 6.00
        2nd, Butter Churn marked "Proctor & Gamble"   30.00-35.00
        3rd, 9½" or 10¼" Straw holder, crystal   20.00-25.00
                           green   55.00-65.00
                           pink   60.00-70.00
        4th, 12" Straw holder, crystal   40.00-45.00
                      green   60.00-70.00
                      pink   65.00-75.00

Row 2: 1st, 5½" Cookie and lid   18.00-20.00
        2nd & 3rd, L.E. Smith, cookie and lid   20.00-22.00
        4th, Hocking green pitcher, 2 qt.   8.00-10.00

Row 3: 1st, Three lip measuring cup marked "Green's Milk, Ice Cream,
        The Cream of York County"   4.00- 6.00
        2nd, McKee decaled blue lady shaker   6.00- 8.00
        3rd, Condiment set, U.S. Glass   30.00-35.00
        4th & 5th, Embossed flour and sugar, ea.   15.00-18.00

Row 4: 1st, "Jennyware", ultra-marine, 36 oz. pitcher   50.00-60.00
        2nd, Ecko Company, Chicago, crystal, 36 oz., pitcher   3.00- 5.00
        3rd, Hazel Atlas "Dot" pitcher, 20 oz.   8.00-10.00
        4th, Delphite (Sunflower bottom design)   18.00-20.00

Row 5: 1st & 2nd, Hazel Atlas fired-on red or blue, 4", 10 oz.   2.00- 3.00
        3rd & 4th, Shakers marked "Tipp City", ea.   1.00- 1.50
        5th, Hazel Atlas, 5", 18 oz.   3.00- 4.00

*Aqua coloring added to help show design.

PART 2
REAMERS, Sunkist, McKee, etc.

Reamers come in many shapes, sizes and colors; and true collectors of these juice extractors take EVERYTHING about them into consideration, i.e., the type of handle, the type of spout, the size of the reaming section, reamer type (lemon, orange or grapefruit), whether they're footed or flat bottomed, whether there is or isn't any embossed lettering on the reamer, whether they have seed dams or not, the colors the particular styles come in, etc! It was never my intention to get totally immeshed in the technicalities regarding reamers. Rather, I intend you should get an overview of the types and colors that various companies made and that you should be made aware of their general worth.

McKee made most of the "Sunkist" reamers which are those most commonly found. All but three of the reamers on the following page were made by McKee.

Row 1:	1st, pink	20.00- 25.00
	2nd, Seville yellow	30.00- 35.00
	3rd, Skokie green, light	15.00- 20.00
Row 2:	1st, Forest green	175.00-225.00
	2nd, Black	235.00-285.00
	3rd, Green (yellowish tint)	12.00- 15.00
Row 3:	1st, Flat white	18.00- 20.00
	2nd, Caramel opalescent	350.00-400.00
	3rd, Green	15.00- 18.00
Row 4:	1st, Chalaine blue	55.00- 65.00
	2nd, Chalaine blue, light	55.00- 65.00
	3rd, Custard	15.00- 20.00
Row 5:	1st, Caramel swirl	100.00-150.00
	2nd, Fry-like, oplescent white	35.00- 40.00
	3rd, Antique white, blocked-in embossing, not McKee	40.00- 45.00
Row 6:	1st, Milk glass, Thatcher Glass	8.00- 10.00
	2nd, Crystal, embossed "Sunkist" in bottom, Federal	150.00-175.00
	3rd, Skokie green, dark	15.00- 20.00

REAMERS, McKEE

Here are a variety of McKee reamers including some grapefruit ones which stand out a mile from the others. The pink grapefruit reamer is quite rare and the blue one directly above it is extremely desireable.

The first two rows show small McKee footed reamers with the first and third of the second row having pointed cones rather than the more rounded type of the others. Those rounded type are embossed " McK "; the pointed ones are not embossed. These pointed reamers are the more desirable to collectors.

On the bottom row, the larger footed reamers both have the " McK " in the circle that is McKee's insignia. That embossing adds a few dollars to the price.

Row 1: 1st, Custard, small, footed, embossed " McK "   16.00- 20.00
        2nd, White, small, footed, embossed " McK "   14.00- 18.00
        Delphite blue, small, footed, embossed, " McK "   150.00-175.00

Row 2: 1st, Custard, small, footed, pointed, not embossed   27.50- 32.50
        2nd, Skokie green, small, footed, embossed " McK "   8.00- 10.00
        3rd, Skokie green, small, footed, pointed, not embossed

Row 3: 1st, Skokie green, grapefruit   60.00- 75.00
        2nd, Chalaine blue, grapefruit   200.00-250.00
        3rd, Seville yellow, grapefruit   185.00-210.00

Row 4: 1st, Custard, large, footed, embossed " McK "   17.50- 20.00
        2nd, Pink, grapefruit   350.00-400.00
        3rd, White (green tinge), large, footed, embossed " McK "   16.00- 18.00

REAMERS, McKEE & FRY

The large McKee reamers on the top row are unembossed and are therefore, slightly less costly. Rows 2, 3 and part of 4 show Fry reamers in both the ruffled top and straight sided variety.

Turned sideways in the 4th row is a "Blue Goose" reamer by Fry. It is embossed "Blue Goose for most juice and finest flavor" and is unusual because of the embossing. The opalescent Fry, without the embossing, is quite common. A close up of the embossing is shown in the inset photograph below.

Row 1:	1st, Large, Skokie green, footed, McKee, unembossed	15.00- 20.00
	2nd, Large, custard, footed, McKee, unembossed	20.00- 25.00
Row 2:	1st, Opalescent, Fry, ruffled top	20.00- 25.00
	2nd, Emerald green, Fry, ruffled top	100.00-125.00
	3rd, Pink, Fry, ruffled top	100.00-125.00
Row 3:	1st, Pink, Fry, straight side	30.00- 35.00
	2nd, Vaseline, Fry, straight side, embossed	125.00-150.00
	2nd, Vaseline, Fry, straight side, unembosed	35.00- 40.00
	3rd, Emerald green, Fry, straight side	30.00- 35.00
	3rd, Light green	10.00- 12.00
Row 4:	1st, Vaseline, Fry, ruffled	125.00-150.00
	2nd, Opalescent, Fry, "Blue Goose" embossing	160.00-185.00
	2nd, Opalescent, Fry, no embossing	8.00- 12.00
	3rd, Amber, unkown maker	100.00-125.00
Row 5:	1st, Green, Rockwell?	45.00- 55.00
	2nd, Pink, Rockwell?	75.00- 85.00

REAMERS, FEDERAL GLASS COMPANY

Federal reamers that are of any monetary importance have been placed on racks for your better scrutiny. In Row 1, the crystal would be very ordinary if it weren't for the "Sunkist" embossed in the bottom.

Row 1:   1st, Crystal, loop handle, "Sunkist" embossing   150.00-175.00
                                 no embossing   2.00-   3.00
          2nd, Amber, loop handle   6.00-   9.00

Row 2:   1st, Green, plain side, tab handle   3.50-   4.00
          2nd, Amber, plain side, tab handle   100.00-125.00
          3rd, Crystal, plain side, tab handle   1.00-   1.50

Row 3:   1st, Pink, ribbed, loop handle   12.00- 15.00
          2nd, White, ribbed, loop handle   4.00-   6.50
          3rd, Amber, ribbed, loop handle   6.00-   9.00

Row 4:   1st, Amber, tab handle, seed dam, ribbed   6.00-   9.00
          2nd, Pink, tab handle, seed dam, ribbed   75.00- 85.00
          3rd, Green, tab handle, seed dam, plain   4.00- 6.00

REAMERS, HAZEL ATLAS

A major problem for beginners is getting the two quart pitchers of Hocking and Hazel Atlas separated. Remember, the Hazel Atlas says "Measuring and Mixing cup" in the bottom of the pitcher whereas Hocking's is just plain.

The "Crisscross" reamers of Row 3 and 4 are avidly sought except in the green color. The tab handle is a lemon reamer and the larger, loop handled "Crisscross" is the orange reamer.

Except for the green in the second row, the pitchers are harder to locate than are the reamers. There is a matching ring of color on the reamer tops for the pitchers in the 1st row.

Row 1: 1st & 2nd, White, 2 quart pitcher & reamer   20.00- 22.00
          3rd "Dots"   25.00- 30.00

Row 2: 1st, Pink, quart pitcher & reamer   100.00-125.00
          2nd, Yellow, quart pitcher & reamer   200.00-250.00
          3rd, Blue, quart pitcher & reamer   125.00-150.00
          4th, Green, quart pitcher & reamer   10.00- 12.00

Row 3: 1st, "Crisscross", green, tab handle, lemon   6.00- 7.00
          2nd, White, red trim ring, tab handle   10.00- 12.00
          2nd, White, plain   5.00- 7.00
          3rd, Green, tab handled, lemon   3.00- 5.00

Row 4: 1st, "Crisscross", orange reamer, loop handle, pink   125.00-150.00
          2nd, "Crisscross", orange reamer, loop handle, crystal   2.00- 3.00
          3rd, "Crisscross", orange reamer, loop handle, blue   100.00-125.00

Row 5: 1st, Tab handle, blue   125.00-150.00
          2nd, Tab handle, pink   10.00- 12.00
          3rd, Tab handle, clambroth   45.00- 55.00
          4th, Tab handle, crystal   1.00- 1.50

REAMERS, HOCKING GLASS COMPANY

In Hocking's catalogue they listed three types of reamers---the tab handled ones were called lemon reamers; the loop handled ones were orange reamers; and pitchers with reamers on top were called fruit juice reamers. (See page 119).

I suspect that reamer collectors looked first at the black reamer on the bottom shelf; alas, it's only sprayed black over crystal. Sorry!

The cornflower blue, or as Depression collectors would say, the "Mayfair" blue reamers are coveted by reamer collectors.

Row 1: 1st, Vitrock, orange reamer (loop handle), embossed   10.00- 12.50
       1st, Vitrock, orange reamer, (loop handle), unembossed   5.00- 6.50
       2nd, Green, 2 quart, fruit juice   12.00- 14.00
       3rd, Blue, orange reamer (loop handle)   200.00-250.00

Row 2: 1st, Green, 1 quart, fruit juice   10.00- 12.50
       2nd, Blue, 1 quart, fruit juice   150.00-175.00
       3rd, Vitrock, 1 quart, fruit juice   12.00- 15.00

Row 3: 1st, Pink, 1 quart, ribbed, fruit juice   65.00- 75.00
       2nd, Green, panelled, orange reamer (loop handle)   4.00- 7.00
       3rd, Vitrock, lemon reamer, tab handle   10.00- 12.00

Row 4: 1st, Green, ribbed, orange reamer (loop handle)   4.00- 7.00
       2nd, Black, flashed-on, orange reamer (loop handle)   8.00- 10.00
       3rd, Coke bottle green, orange reamer (loop handle)   7.50- 10.00

REAMERS, JEANNETTE

    The bucket reamers on the top shelf of the picture are Hex Optic pattern. The first two reamers in Row 2 are "Jennyware". Those small tab handled reamers on Row 2 have seed dams.
    The dark Jadite color is harder to find and therefore brings a premium price.

Row 1: 'Hex Optic' bucket reamer, green	15.00-17.50
pink	17.50-20.00
Row 2: 1st & 2nd, "Jennyware", crystal	45.00-55.00
pink	40.00-47.50
ultramarine	40.00-50.00
3rd & 4th, Small, tab handled, green	25.00-30.00
pink	37.50-42.50
Row 3: 1st, Light jadite	6.00- 9.00
2nd, Dark jadite	18.00-22.00
3rd, Delphite	20.00-25.00
Row 4: 1st & 2nd, Large, tab handled, green or pink	30.00-35.00
3rd & 4th, Green	6.00- 9.00
Light jadite	9.00-12.00
Dark jadite	25.00-30.00
Row 5: 1st & 3rd, Pitcher w/reamer, dark jadite	30.00-35.00
light jadite	15.00-20.00
translucent green	40.00-50.00
2nd, Crystal	4.00- 6.00

REAMERS, MANNY AND EASLEY

I quote one serious reamer collector's reaction upon seeing this picture, "Oh, all that crystal garbage!"

These all fit nicely into that category and **range in price from $.50 - $2.00** on a good day. I will, however, dutifully tell you of all the embossings and price only those worth more.

Row 1:   1st, "Manny, Pat. Aug 25, 1885; Nov 12, 1886; 2 Pats. Dec 2 '90; June '29;
           July 30, '09"
           2nd, unembossed
           3rd, unembossed, tab handle

Row 2:   1st, "Easley's New Model May 11, 1909 No. 4", $5.00-6.00
           2nd, "Easley's improved patent Mar. 6, 1900, $4.00-5.00
           3rd, Thumbprint type reamer, "Easley pat. Pend.", $40.00-45.00

Row 3:   1st, "Easley's improv'd, Mar. 6, 1900"
           2nd, "Easley pat. July 10, 1888; Sep. 10, 1889", $14.00-16.00
           3rd, unembossed
           4th, "Easley pat. July 10, 1888; Sep. 10, 1889"

Row 4:   1st, unembossed
           2nd, "Easley pat. July 10th, 1888", $12.00-14.00
           3rd, "Easleys July 10, 1888; Sep. 10, 1889"
           4th, unembossed

JUICE EXTRACTOR

1 C928—Opal Glass, 5¾ in., lipped,
patent cone, improved seed catcher.
3 doz. in carton, 30 lbs.
Doz 75c

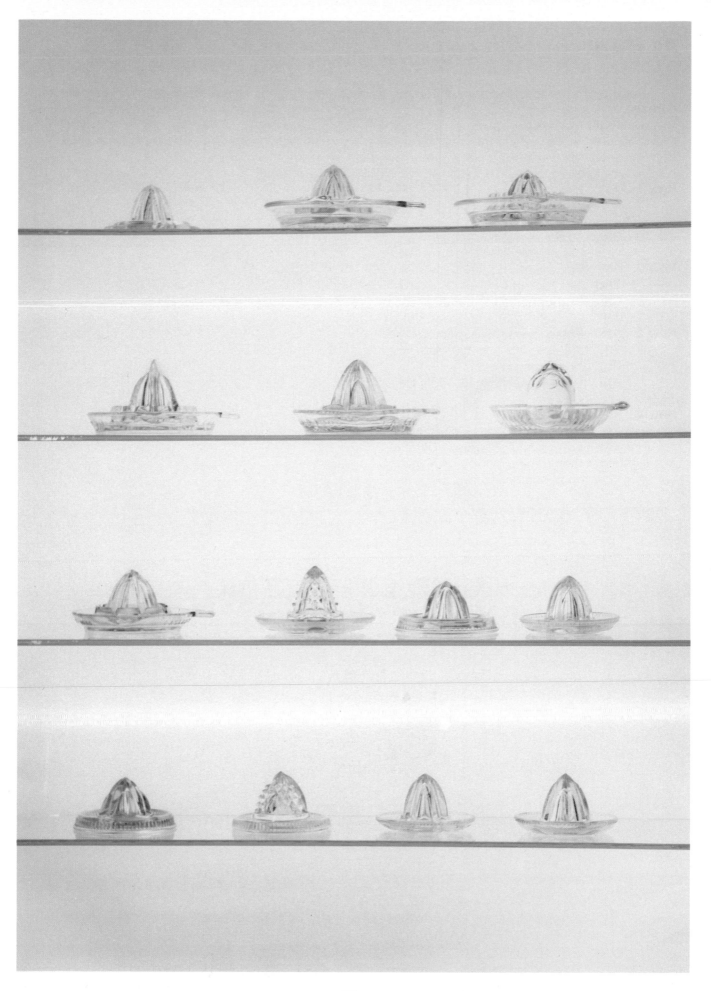

Reamers by U.S. Glass shown here all have one characteristic in common---their reamer fits a pitcher or container of some sort. None of these are very expensive except the white one in the 3rd Row.

The reamer and pitcher at the end of Row 2 are mismatched pointing out the problem of finding like colors when buying the pieces independently of each other.

Most all pitchers have a ledge on which to seat the reamer.

Row 1:	1st, Green, snow flake design in bottom, 4 cup container	20.00-22.00
	2nd, Green, Handy Andy	25.00-30.00
	3rd, Green, Servmor (slick handle type)	40.00-55.00
Row 2:	1st, Pink, etched	20.00-25.00
	2nd, Turquoise (slick handle)	28.00-30.00
	3rd, Frosted green (slick handle)	18.00-22.00
	4th, Green, (w/matching colors)	20.00-25.00
Row 3:	1st, Crystal, w/flowers	10.00-12.00
	2nd, Pink w/fruit	20.00-25.00
	3rd, White	55.00-65.00
Row 4:	1st, Pink, frosted (slick handle)	20.00-22.00
	2nd, Green (slick handle)	15.00-20.00
	3rd, Turquoise	20.00-25.00
	4th, Pink (slick handle)	20.00-25.00
Row 5:	1st, Green (slick handle)	15.00-20.00
	2nd, Green	15.00-20.00
	3rd, Pink with etching	20.00-25.00
	4th, Green (slick handle)	18.00-20.00

ORANGE REAMER SET

I C774—2 piece, crystal or green glass, **1 pt. pitcher,** 3¼ in. high, 4¾ in. diam., ½ cup graduation, **removable cone reamer.**

Doz $2.00

REAMERS, WESTMORELAND, PADEN CITY AND POSSIBLY FENTON

The pitchers on the top row are Westmoreland and were turned hoping the camera would pick up the lemon and orange designs embossed into either side of the pitchers. These are not commonly found.

The 3rd and 4th row of reamers have been attributed to Paden City; however, those in Row 4 appear to have many characteristics and color varieties of the Fenton Glass Company.

Cocktail shaker reamers appear unique to Paden City. The metal insert is hard to find and the shaker part is difficult to sell without that part.

Row 1: 1st, Green, lemon/orange, Westmoreland	100.00-125.00
2nd, Pink, lemon/orange, Westmoreland	110.00-135.00
Row 2: 1st, Pink, Westmoreland, flattened loop handle	40.00- 50.00
2nd, Crystal, decorated flattened loop handle	25.00- 30.00
3rd, Green, Westmoreland, flattened loop handle	75.00- 80.00
Row 3: 1st, Pink, Paden City, shaker type w/metal insert	30.00- 35.00
2nd, Green, Paden City, 2 quart, etched, complete	95.00-110.00
3rd, Pink, Paden City, 2 quart, etched, complete	95.00-110.00
4th, Amber, Paden City, shaker type, complete	40.00- 50.00
Row 4: 1st, Black top, Fenton?	75.00-100.00
Pitcher, black	125.00-150.00
Reamer complete	200.00-250.00
2nd, Red top (reamer), Fenton?	100.00-125.00
Pitcher, red	175.00-200.00
Reamer, complete	250.00-300.00
4th, Green top (reamer), Fenton?	50.00- 60.00
Pitcher, green	100.00-125.00
Reamer complete	150.00-200.00

REAMERS, UNKNOWN, SOME WEST COAST

If you look closely at the tomato slag reamer in the second row you can see the Fleur-de-Lis symbol from which the two red reamers take their name.

Notice the slick handled white reamer in the third row.

The markings on the reamers in the last row are as follows: pink, "Lindsey"; crystal, "Sunkist -California Fruit Growers Exchange, L.A."; and the last crystal one is marked "Sunkist Oranges and Lemons".

Row 1: 1st, Green, tab handle   10.00- 12.50
        2nd, Pink   35.00- 40.00
        3rd, Green   25.00- 30.00

Row 2: 1st, Red slag, "Fleur-de-Lis"   200.00-250.00
        2nd, Red slag, "Fleur-de-Lis"   200.00-250.00
        3rd, White milk glass   35.00- 40.00

Row 3: 1st, Milk glass, slick handle   45.00- 50.00
        2nd, Milk white, "Valencia" embossed   50.00- 60.00
        3rd, Trans. Green, "Valencia" embossed   100.00-125.00

Row 4: 1st, Pink, "Lindsey" embossed   200.00-250.00
        2nd, Crystal, "California Fruit Growers - Sunkist"   15.00- 18.00
        3rd, Crystal, "Sunkist Oranges & Lemons"   15.00- 18.00

REAMERS, MISCELLANEOUS

In the second row, there are two opalescent blue lemon reamers which are not commonly found. The one at the left is very close to Duncan Miller blue.

"Radnt" is prominently embossed on the large crystal reamer in the center.

By far the most interesting reamer on this page is the bead bottomed cobalt blue one shown in Row 4. It's a Cambridge reamer marked "Pat. Jan. 6, 1909" and it was heretofore known only in crystal.

At the bottom, the hand reamer is embossed "Little handy lemon squeezor - Silver & Co., N.Y. -Pat applied for". The Mexican hat shaped one next to it is marked "Ideal - pat'd Jan. 31, '88".

Black reamers are not that easily found anyway, but the OVAL black top pictured is doubly hard. The last crystal reamer is marked "Cambridge - pat'd #912443".

Row 1:	1st, Green, tab handle	10.00- 12.50
	2nd, Green, Jenkins Glass Co., short, tab handle (rare in green)	40.00- 50.00
	Crystal	8.00- 10.00
	3rd, Green, yellow tint, tab handle	2.50- 4.00
Row 2:	1st, Blue opalescent (like Duncan Miller blue)	100.00-125.00
	2nd, Blue opalescent	100.00-125.00
	3rd, Crystal, platinum trim	25.00- 30.00
Row 3:	1st, White	25.00- 35.00
	2nd, Crystal "Radnt"	50.00- 65.00
	3rd, Crystal, swirl side	30.00- 35.00
Row 4:	1st, Clambroth	75.00- 85.00
	2nd, Blue, Cambridge, "Pat. Jan. 6, 1909"	300.00-350.00
	3rd, Crystal	8.00- 10.00
Row 5:	1st, Crystal, hand reamer "Little handy lemon squeezer"	45.00- 55.00
	2nd, Crystal, Ideal, "pat'd Jan. 31, '88"	100.00-125.00
	3rd, Black reamer top, oval	125.00-150.00
	4th, Crystal, Cambridge	10.00- 15.00

REAMERS, CRYSTAL, MOSTLY UNKNOWN ORIGIN

The weird shaped reamer in the second row was made in Czechoslovakia; other than that, these are unmarked, unknown and of little interest to collectors. We HAD them available, so we included them. I haven't seen too many of the two piece reamers like the one at the bottom at the shows I've attended.

Row 1: 1st, Crystal, pitcher reamer   5.00- 7.50
            2nd, Crystal, loop handle   1.50- 2.00
            3rd, Crystal, loop handle   10.00-12.50

Row 2: 1st, Crystal, Czechoslavakia   35.00-45.00
            2nd, Crystal, tab handle   2.00- 2.50
            3rd, Crystal, tab handle   2.00- 2.50

Row 3: 1st, Crystal, tab handle   2.00- 2.50
            2nd, Crystal, tab handle   2.00- 2.50
            3rd, Crystal, tab handle   2.00- 2.50

Row 4: 1st, Crystal, tab handle   2.00- 2.50
            2nd, Crystal, tab handle   10.00-12.00
            3rd, Crystal, 2 piece, no spout   15.00-20.00

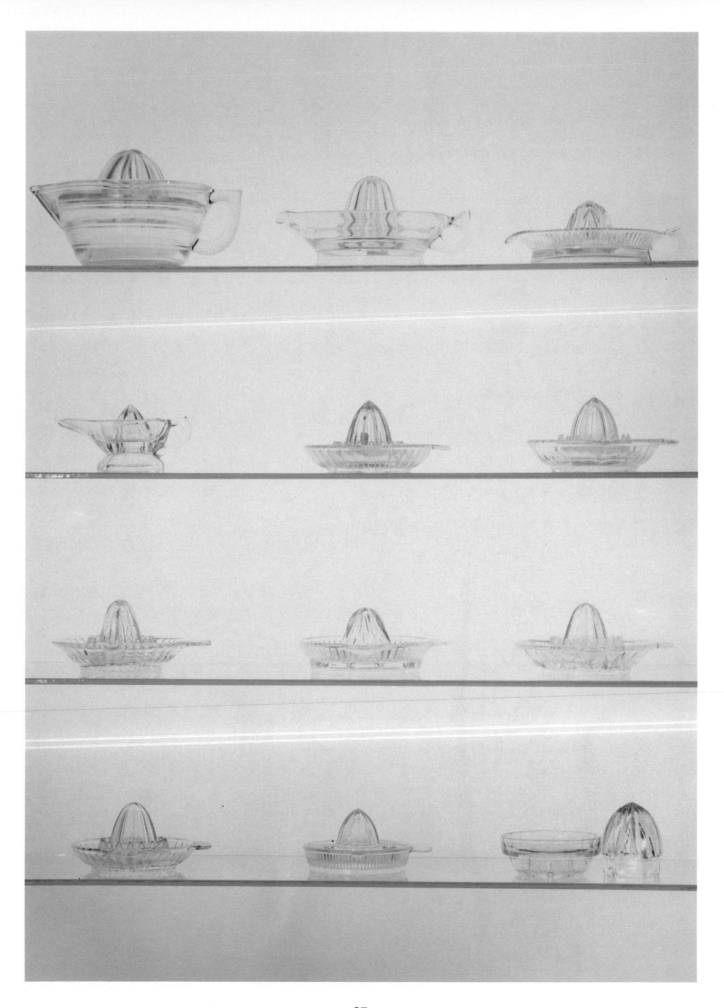

REAMERS

Noteworthy here are the black amethyst "orange juice extractor" in Row 2 and the two Tufglas reamers in the center of the bottom row. That Coke bottle green color I have found out is the standard color gotten when glass is chemically made. The manufacturer has to "kill" this natural color of glass before making crystal or colors.

Row 1: 1st, Crystal, "Orange Juice Extractor"   20.00- 25.00
        2nd, Light green, "Orange Juice Extractor"   30.00- 40.00
        3rd, Pink, "Orange Juice Extractor"   50.00- 60.00

Row 2: 1st, Black amethyst, "Orange Juice Extractor"   150.00-175.00
        2nd, Green, "Orange Juice Extractor"   35.00- 45.00

Row 3: 1st, Crystal, tab handle, "Orange Juice Extractor"   10.00- 12.00
        2nd, Crystal, round handle, "Orange Juice Extractor"   10.00- 12.00
        3rd, Green, tab handle, "Orange Juice Extractor"   15.00- 20.00

Row 4: 1st, Crystal, "Orange Juice Extractor"   12.00- 15.00
        2nd, Crystal, "Orange Juice Extractor"   12.00- 15.00
        3rd, White   30.00- 35.00

Row 5: 1st, Crystal, tab handle   10.00- 15.00
        2nd, Tufglas, light green   70.00- 80.00
        3rd, Tufglas, dark green   70.00- 80.00
        4th, Same as 1st, green   35.00- 40.00

Fruit Reamer
Made of pressed green glass with grooved cone center. Cleanly extracts all of juice from fruit.
Not Prepaid.   Shpg. wt., 3 lbs.
35 E 585—Each.............9c

98

REAMERS, TWO PIECE

Even if you aren't into reamer collecting per se, you'll have to admit that several of these on this page would be fun to have on a shelf at home!

Row 1: 1st & 2nd, White, two handle w/rabbit (top only: $8.00-10.00)   65.00-76.00
          1st & 2nd, White, two handle, plain   25.00-35.00
          3rd, Pink, complete   60.00-75.00

Row 2: 1st, Ice blue   65.00-75.00
          2nd, Crystal   10.00-12.00
          3rd, Frosted   15.00-20.00
          3rd, Frosted w/chicks   45.00-55.00

Row 3: 1st, Crystal, block style, w/trim   15.00-20.00
          2nd, Pink, tab handle   45.00-50.00
          3rd, Green, Jenkins Glass Co.   65.00-70.00
          3rd, Crystal   15.00-20.00

Row 4: 1st, Crystal, two handled   10.00-12.00
          2nd, Crystal, two handled   10.00-12.00
          3rd, Crystal, one handle   25.00-35.00

REAMERS, UNUSUAL

These three reamers were separated from the others because of their unusual style or uniqueness.

You may have noticed the mechanical green reamer on the cover. It was made to be attached to the edge of the old kitchen cabinet. As the handle was turned, the cone also turned and this extracted the juice. Unfortunately, it was still a two hand operation.

The black amethyst Saunders reamer has the most pointed cone of any pictured in the book. It seems possible that using it too vigorously might be dangerous to your hand. This reamer is considered quite a find for reamer collectors.

As of this writing, the Cambridge blue reamer, dated "Jan. 6, 1909" is one-of-a-kind. I'd appreciate hearing about any others you may find.

1st, Mechanical green reamer w/attachment feature	100.00-125.00
2nd, Cambridge reamer, blue	400.00-450.00
jade green	300.00-350.00
3rd, Saunders reamer, black	300.00-350.00

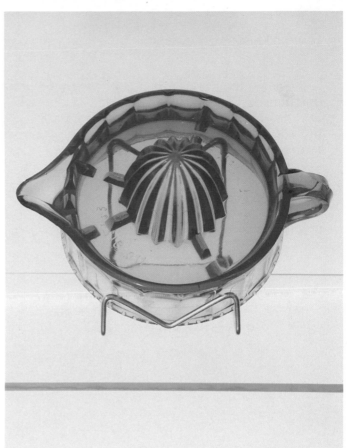

PART 3

ALL PROVEN SELLERS

PANTRY, REFRIGERATOR AND MIXING BOWL SETS

A. G151—8-PCE. GREEN PANTRY SET

Set consists of
Four G526 Jars w/ Glass Covers
(Labelled Sugar, Flour, Cereal and Coffee)
Four G523 Jars, Aluminum Tops
(Labelled Spice, Sugar, Salt and Pepper)
1 Set in Carton, 10½ lbs.

Every housewife will appreciate this Set. It's one thing that will materially help to keep order in the pantry or kitchen. "A place for everything and everything in its place." Made of a delicate Green Glass with black and silver colored labels, it adds color as well as convenience to any household. Order 25 or 50 sets, fill up your window with the cartons, make a mass display, show one set unpacked and you'll be surprised with its appeal.

B. G148—6-PCE. GREEN REFRIGERATOR SET

Set consists of one each
G31 6" Oval Refrig. Jar & Cover
G33 7" Oval Refrig. Jar & Cover
G35 8" Oval Refrig. Jar & Cover
1 Set in Carton, 7 lbs.

A very necessary accessory to your Refrigerator. These money saving covered Jars preserve food and conserve space. Just the thing for left overs, salads, butter, sandwich fillings and other foods that must be kept for several days. All Jars have convenient recessed knobs in Covers. Jars can be stacked one upon the other if desired. These Sets can be most effectively used as sale closers with Refrigerator purchasers. A set costs but little but accomplishes wonderful results for you.

C. G149—5-PCE. GREEN MIXING BOWL SET

Set consists of one each
6½" Green Glass Mixing Bowl
7½" Green Glass Mixing Bowl
8½" Green Glass Mixing Bowl
9½" Green Glass Mixing Bowl
10½" Green Glass Mixing Bowl
1 Set in Carton, 10 lbs.

These Green Mixing Bowls have rolled edge and self balancing features. The Rolled Edge affords a convenient hand grip and prevents chipping. The bottom construction of these Bowls causes them, when tipped to rest in a suitable position for mixing. They will not roll from side to side, as the ordinary Mixing Bowl does. The side panels aid in holding the Bowl and are quite decorative. These Bowls are highly polished and a delightful accessory to any kitchen.

HOCKING GLASS COMPANY

9

KITCHEN GLASSWARE

BEST SELLERS IN KITCHEN WARE

REF.	ITEM NO.	DESCRIPTION	SIZE	DOZ. CTN.	WT. CTN.
A	G10	Green Measuring Cup	8 oz.	4	34 lb
B	G1	Green Caster Cup	1⅝"	12	30 lb
	1	Crystal Caster Cup	1⅝"	12	30 lb
	G2	Green Caster Cup	2¼"	12	44 lb
	2	Crystal Caster Cup	2¼"	12	44 lb
C	G101	Green Ash Tray	4¼"	4	30 lb
	101	Crystal Ash Tray	4¼"	4	30 lb
D	G31	Green Syrup T. T.	9 oz.	2	28 lb
	31	Crystal Syrup T. T.	9 oz.	2	28 lb
E	G30	Green Salt & Pepper A. T.	3¼"	12	27 lb
	30	Crystal Salt & Pepper A. T.	3¼"	12	27 lb
F	G5	Green Percolator Top	2¼"	12	28 lb
	5	Crystal Percolator Top	2¼"	12	28 lb
G	G638	Green Measuring Jug	16 oz.	4	67 lb
	G8	Green Extractor	5¼"	4	38 lb
H	G571	Green Cookie Jar Green Cap	1 Gal.	1	48 lb
I	G28	Green Sqr. Refrig. Jar & Cvr.	5"	2	55 lb

REF.	ITEM NO.	DESCRIPTION	SIZE	DOZ. CTN.	WT. CTN.
K	G33	Green Oval Refrig. Jar & Cvr.	7"	2	54 lb
L	G994	Green Sanitary Butter & Cvr.	1 lb.	2	50 lb
M	G601	Green Refrig. Bottle & Cap	32 oz.	2	38 lb
	G602	Green Refrig. Bottle & Cap	62 oz.	1	29 lb
N	G505	Green Mixing Bowl	6½"	3	29 lb
	G506	Green Mixing Bowl	7¼"	3	37 lb
	G507	Green Mixing Bowl	8¼"	2	36 lb
	G508	Green Mixing Bowl	9¼"	2	50 lb
	G509	Green Mixing Bowl	10¼"	1	33 lb
	G510	Green Mixing Bowl	11¼"	1	41 lb
P	G13	Green Fruit Juice Extractor	6"	3	38 lb
Q	G523	Green Salt A. T.	3¼ oz.	2	13 lb
	G523	Green Pepper A. T.	3¼ oz.	2	13 lb
R	G526	Green Coffee Jar & Cover	47 oz.	2	48 lb
	G526	Green Sugar Jar & Cover	47 oz.	2	48 lb
	G526	Green Cereal Jar & Cover	47 oz.	2	48 lb
	G526	Green Flour Jar & Cover	47 oz.	2	48 lb

G13 Green Kitchenware Deal

G13 Reamer

G308—8" Mixing Bowl

G31 Can T. T.

G23 Refrigerator
Jar and Cover

G994 Butter
and Cover

G501 Refrigerator Bottle
With Black Enameled Cap

G640 Measuring Jug

G653—56 oz. Jug

G293 Water Chiller and
Stopper

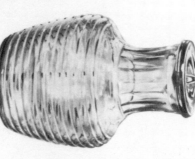

THE HOCKING GLASS CO., LANCASTER, OHIO

HOCKING GLASS COMPANY

13

G14 Green Kitchenware Deal

Two G20 Jars and Covers
One G21 Jar and Cover

G680—80 oz. Jug

G306—6"
G307—7"
G308—8"

G174 Cookie Jar

G523

G515

G523

G525

G524

G525

THE HOCKING GLASS CO., LANCASTER, OHIO

HOCKING GLASS COMPANY

107

The Hocking Glass Co., Lancaster, Ohio

GREEN KITCHEN WARE

G535—Coffee Jar A. C.

G534 Tea Jar A. C.

G533—Spice Jar A. C.

G533—Salt and Pepper A. T.

G ½ Pt. Provision Jar and Cover

G 1 Pt. Provision Jar and Cover

G 1 Qt—Provision Jar and Cover

G 2 Qt—Provision Jar and Cover

G—501—Water Bottle A. C.

G640—Jug and G8—Reamer

G638—Measuring Jug and G8—Reamer

G10—Measuring Cup

G15—5" Refrigerator Jar and Cover

G17—7" Refrigerator Jar and Cover

G19—9" Refrigerator Jar and Cover

G293—Water Chiller and Cover

G5—Reamer

G9—Reamer

G23—Refrigerator Jar and Cover

G991—Refrigerator Jar and Cover

G992—Butter and Cover

G21—Refrigerator Jar and Cover

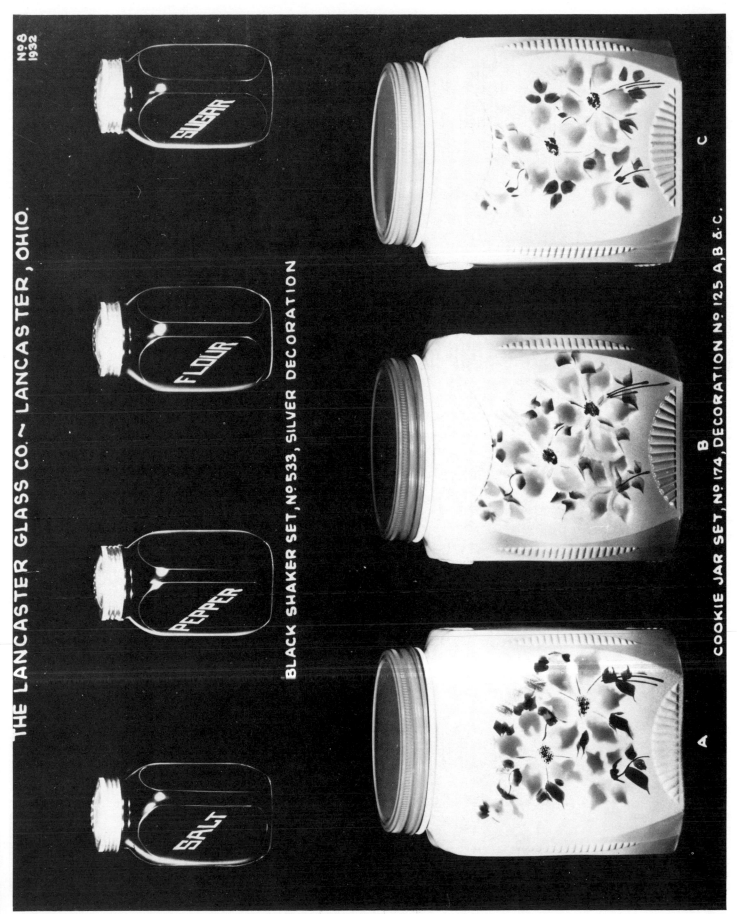

THE LANCASTER GLASS CO. ~ LANCASTER, OHIO.

No 8
1932

SALT

PEPPER

FLOUR

SUGAR

BLACK SHAKER SET, No 533, SILVER DECORATION

A

B

C

COOKIE JAR SET, No 174, DECORATION No 125 A, B & C.

LANCASTER GLASS COMPANY

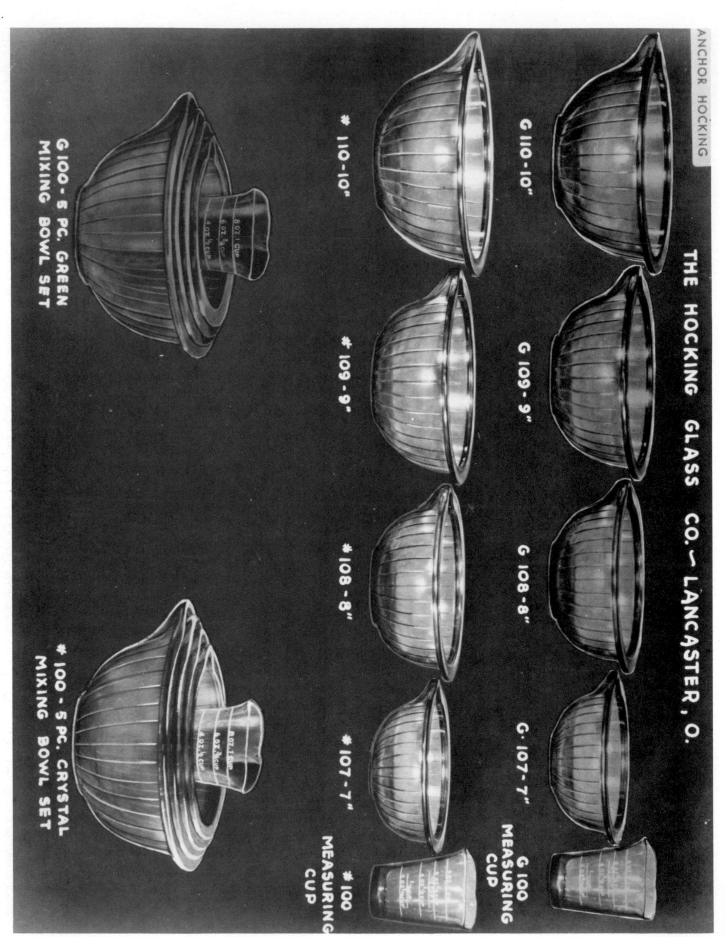

THE HOCKING GLASS CO. ~ LANCASTER, O.

G 110-10"

110-10"

G 100-5 PC. GREEN
MIXING BOWL SET

G 109-9"

109-9"

G 108-8"

108-8"

G-107-7"

107-7"

G 100
MEASURING
CUP

100
MEASURING
CUP

100-5 PC. CRYSTAL
MIXING BOWL SET

HOCKING GLASS COMPANY

110

THE HOCKING GLASS CO. — LANCASTER, OHIO.

12-PC. KITCHEN SET

ONE - G7 REFRIGERATOR JAR & COVER
ONE - G9 REFRIGERATOR JAR & COVER
ONE - G10 MEASURING CUP
ONE - G 109 - 9" MIXING BOWL
SIX - G 901 TUMBLERS

HOCKING GLASS COMPANY

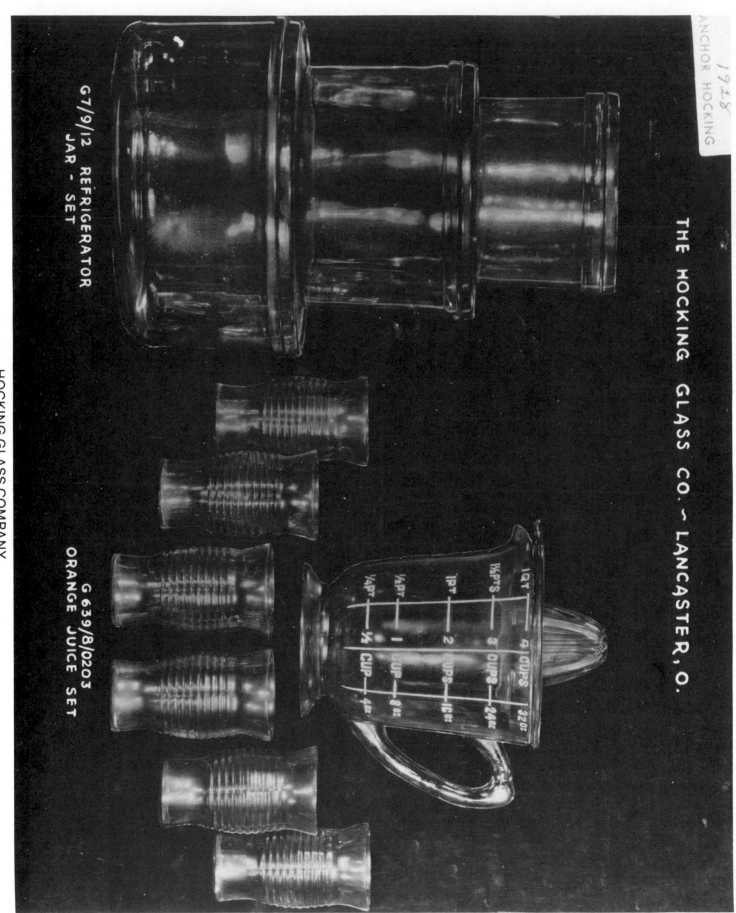

G7/9/12 REFRIGERATOR
JAR - SET

THE HOCKING GLASS CO. ~ LANCASTER, O.

1928

G 639/8/0203
ORANGE JUICE SET

HOCKING GLASS COMPANY

THE HOCKING GLASS CO. LANCASTER, O.

10
CRACKER
JAR

4 PT.
JUG

32 CREAM
0729½ PLATE

31
SYRUP

1 SALT
BOX CPT

3 MEAS.
CUP

4 PERCO   1 PERCO
TOP DEC1 CRYSTAL

4 PERCO
DEC 3

17
OIL

2
CUSPIDOR
DEC 200

6
CASTER REAMER   REAMER

2
CASTER REAMER

ROLLING PIN

5 PC.
MIX BOWL

5 PC.
REFRIG SET

410
JUG

409
JUG

HOCKING GLASS COMPANY

113

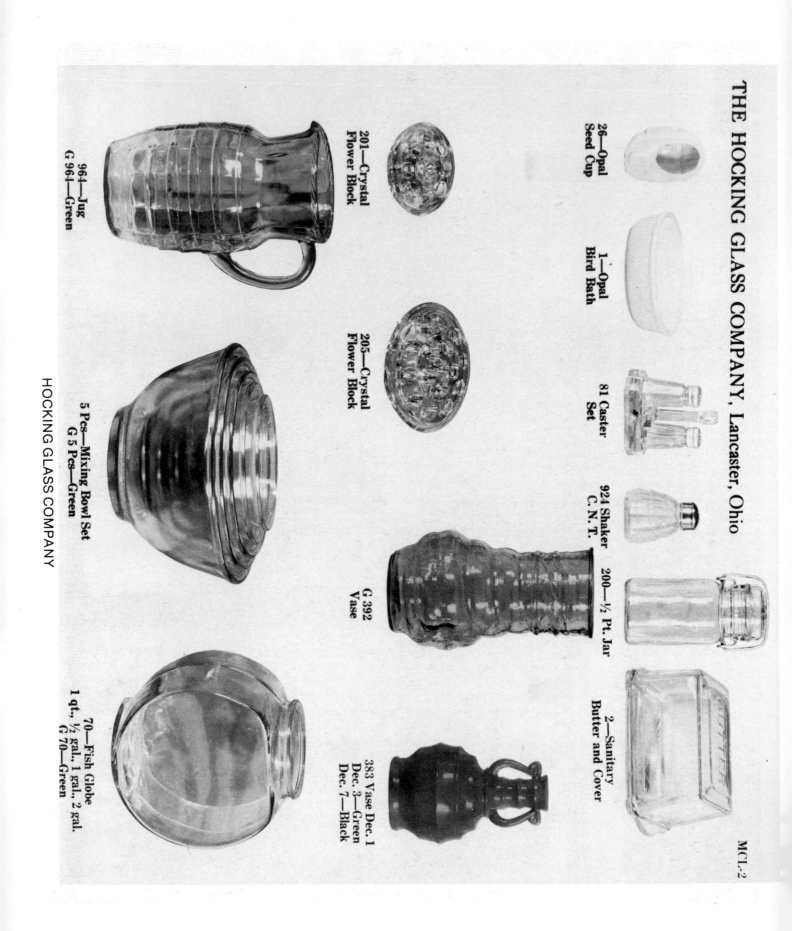

THE HOCKING GLASS COMPANY, Lancaster, Ohio

26—Opal
Seed Cup

1—Opal
Bird Bath

81 Caster
Set

924 Shaker
C. N. T.

200—½ Pt. Jar

2—Sanitary
Butter and Cover

201—Crystal
Flower Block

205—Crystal
Flower Block

G 392
Vase

383 Vase Dec. 1
Dec. 3—Green
Dec. 7—Black

964—Jug
G 964—Green

5 Pcs—Mixing Bowl Set
G 5 Pcs—Green

70—Fish Globe
1 qt., ½ gal., 1 gal., 2 gal.
G 70—Green

MCL-2

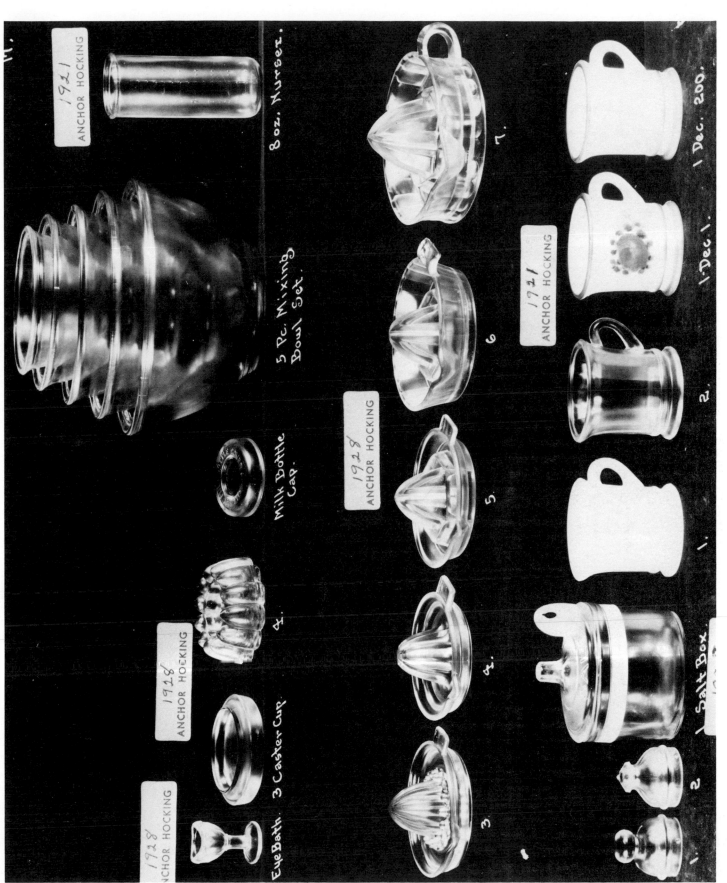

HOCKING GLASS COMPANY

115

HOCKING GLASS COMPANY

5.

13.

4.

19.

8.

4.

7.

26.

28.

24.

27.

20.

"VITROCK" Kitchen Bowls

NO. HW356—3 PIECE BOWL SET

1 each: 6", 7½" and 9" Bowls Plain and Colored as illustrated. Packed 4 doz. sets in ctns. wt. 108 lbs.

	List
Less Carton Lots	$.78 Set
Full Carton Lots	.72 Set

"VITROCK" Range Jars and Kitchen Shakers

NO. HW324R—30 OZ. RANGE JAR & COVER

Packed 2 doz. ctn. wt. 28 lbs.

	List
Less Carton Lots	$2.64 Doz.
Full Carton Lots	2.40 Doz.

NO. HW323R—9 OZ. SALT & PEPPER SHAKERS—Dec. Red

Pkd. 1 doz. prs. ctn. wt. 11 lbs.

	List
Less Carton Lots	$3.60 Doz. Pr.
Full Carton Lots	3.28 Doz. Pr.

NO. HW324B—30 OZ. RANGE JAR & COVER

Packed 2 doz. ctn. wt. 28 lbs.

	List
Less Carton Lots	$2.64 Doz.
Full Carton Lots	2.40 Doz.

NO. HW323B—9 OZ. SALT & PEPPER SHAKERS—Dec. Blue

Pkd. 1 doz. prs. ctn. wt. 11 lbs.

	List
Less Carton Lots	$3.60 Doz. Pr.
Full Carton Lots	3.28 Doz. Pr.

The Reason for This Catalog . . .

Glassware for kitchen, table and gift use, always attracts women. They are constantly buying new pieces! Glassware seems to be a "natural" for Hardware Store use as a Traffic Bringer.

To help you keep your stock up to date on the new glass pieces, this catalog has been prepared. We hope to continue sending you new catalogs 3 or 4 times a year.

Only proven staple sellers or the best of the new items are shown.

To get volume sales keep your stock well displayed.

8   **HALL HARDWARE COMPANY, MINNEAPOLIS, MINN.**   Feb.. 1938

VITROCK KITCHENWARE

VITROCK Kitchenware, with its beautiful white color, reflects cleanliness and will add an undeniable charm to the kitchen equipment of your patrons. The modern vogue in kitchen stoves and ranges, electric and gas refrigerators, porcelain sinks and drain boards, naturally causes housewives to seek the most beautiful mixing bowls, seasoning shakers, refrigerator jars, and fruit juice extractors that they can buy. VITROCK admirably fills this need.

Every merchant should display and price VITROCK Kitchenware AS SETS as well as individual pieces. Your patrons will buy complete Range Sets rather than single shakers, Mixing Bowl Sets rather than individual bowls, if you offer them and push them AS SETS.

Extra Special Range Set - Our V400 Ass't.

24	W523 Salt Shakers—To retail @ 10c		$2.40
24	W523 Pepper Shakers—To retail @ 10c		2.40
24	W515 Drip. Jar & Cov.—To retail @ 15c		3.60
			$8.40
	Costs you only		4.00
	Your profit		**$4.40**

Suggest special retail price 29c per set.

Open Stock

			DOZ. TO CTN.	WGT. PER CTN.	NET PRICE PER DOZ.
W505	6½"	Mixing Bowls	3	29 lbs.	.45
W506	7½"	" "	3	40 "	.78
W507	8½"	" "	2	36 "	.88
W508	9½"	" "	2	47 "	1.30
W509	10½"	" "	1	31 "	1.60
W510	11½"	" "	1	39 "	2.25
W13		Orange Reamers	2	39 "	1.10
W47		Left-over Jar and Cover	2	32 "	.95
W523		Salt-Pepper-Sugar Flour and Spice	2	20 "	.50
W515		Dripping Jar and Cover	2	38 "	1.10
W39		Egg Cups	4	27 "	.60
W49		Ash Trays	2	18 "	.65

Quantities less than those mentioned above—10% advance

W47—LEFTOVER DISH & COVER
Pkd. 2 doz. ctn.—wt. 30 lbs.

W31—6" OVAL REFRIGERATOR
JAR & COVER
Pkd. 2 doz. ctn.—wt. 29 lbs.

W33—7" OVAL REFRIGERATOR
JAR & COVER
Pkd. 2 doz. ctn.—wt. 55 lbs.

W35—8" OVAL REFRIGERATOR
JAR & COVER
Pkd. 1 doz. ctn.—wt. 44 lbs.

W147—BOWL
Pkd. 6 doz. ctn.—wt. 62 lbs.

W657—4" SQUARE
REFRIGERATOR JAR & COVER
Pkd. 3 doz. ctn.—wt. 44 lbs.

W658—4"x8" SQUARE
REFRIGERATOR JAR & COVER
Pkd. 2 doz. ctn.—wt. 60 lbs.

W659—8" SQUARE
REFRIGERATOR JAR & COVER
Pkd. 1 doz. ctn.—wt. 58 lbs.

W13—ORANGE REAMER
Pkd. 2 doz. ctn.—wt. 39 lbs.

W14—LEMON REAMER
Pkd. 4 doz. ctn.—wt. 46 lbs.

W688—1 PINT PITCHER
Pkd. 2 doz. ctn.—wt. 26 lbs.

W8—FRUIT JUICE REAMER
Pkd. 2 doz. ctn.—wt. 20 lbs.

W515—DRIPPINGS JAR
& COVER
Pkd. 2 doz. ctn.—wt. 33 lbs.
W523—SALT SHAKER
Aluminum Top
Pkd. 2 doz. ctn.—wt. 14 lbs.
W523—PEPPER—2 doz. ctn.
W523—SPICE—2 doz. ctn.
W523—SUGAR—2 doz. ctn.
W523—FLOUR—2 doz. ctn.

Rich Looking White Enamel Or Golden Oak Kitchen Cabinet

This strictly high grade kitchen cabinet is furnished in either golden oak or all white enamel, as you prefer. Has all the labor saving features of the higher priced cabinets, with solid oak construction in the golden oak cabinet, and selected cabinet hardwood in the white enamel style.

Get It on Month's Free Trial Loan

OAK CABINET is made of solid oak, carefully planed and sanded until it is perfectly smooth and it is then given three coats of shellac and varnish, making it absolutely water-proof and steam-proof. The finish is a natural golden oak color.

THE WHITE ENAMEL CABINET is made of the finest kind of hardwood and then given several coats of especially prepared snow white enamel that is absolutely moisture-proof and can be washed like a dish.

THE UPPER SECTION On the left-hand side of the upper section is a tilting flour bin with a handy sifter bottom. This flour bin has a capacity of 40 lbs. of flour. Alongside of the flour bin is a roomy compartment, divided in the middle by a shelf. This makes a good place to keep kitchen dinnerware, and the upper shelf can be used for keeping cereals and other things you require in your kitchen work. This section closes with a double door, well fitted and absolutely dust-

THE BASE SECTION On the right-hand side of the base section are two shallow drawers for kitchen cutlery and table linens. Below this is a metal lined drawer with sliding top, for keeping bread, cake and pastries. It is absolutely vermin-proof and will keep your bakery goods fresh and pure. On the left-hand side is a large compartment for keeping pots and pans. It is divided with a wire rack. This closes with a well fitting door, fitted with a wire rack for holding lids and shallow vessels. The cabinet is set high enough from the floor so that you can easily sweep under it. The legs are fitted with easy rolling casters. All of the hardware and metal work is of the best quality, securely fastened.

The cabinet is 70 in. high over all. The work table is 33 in. high from the and the width over all is about 42 in. Shipped from factory in Indiana. ping weight, about 240 lbs.

DAYS' LOAN We will gladly send you this handsome kitchen cabinet on 30 days' free loan so that you can actually use it in home and see how you like it. See the number of steps it saves you daily w much easier it is to do your work.

proof. Below this is a full length section that closes with sliding doors like a roll top desk. This roll curtain door enables you to open and close the compartment without moving any of the things you may have on the table top. You will find it to be quite an advantage. It contains a seven-piece Colonial glass set consisting of a tea jar, coffee jar, spice jars and 10-lb. capacity sugar jar. There is a wire rack in the center to hold the small spice jars and hooks below to hold a rolling pin. The entire upper compartment is finished in pure snow white enamel, easy to keep clean and sanitary.

SLIDING WORK TABLE This table is 42 in. wide and 25 in. deep when closed, and can be pulled out to give you a working space 34 in. deep x 42 in. wide. This work table can be furnished in either shining nickeloid metal or white porcelain, as you prefer. The edges of the porcelain top are slightly raised so that anything spilled on it will not run off onto the floor.

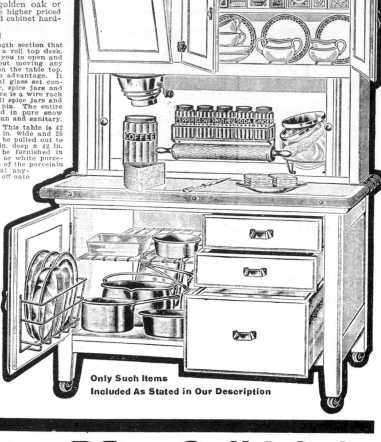

Only Such Items Included As Stated in Our Description

Golden Oak Model

4GB106. | No. 34GB107.
l Cabinet, **$30.95** | Kitchen Cabinet, **$35.95**
ickeloid | with white porcelain
top. Price. | lain top. Price...

All White Enamel Model

We can also furnish this cabinet in all white enamel on the outside and interior of top section white enameled.

9.34GB110. | No. 34GB111.
itchen Cabinet, **$33.85** | Kitchen Cabinet, **$38.95**
h nickeloid | with white porce-
top. Price.. | lain top. Price...

No Money Down

Solid Oak
Kitchen Cabinet

This cabinet is made especially for long service being constructed of solid selected Indiana white oak throughout. The material has been thoroughly air and kiln dried before being used, so that it will not warp, check or split under any conditions. The finish is a rich golden color. The varnish used is water-proof so that it is not effected by the action of steam or moisture in the kitchen. The interior of the top section is finished in white enamel.

The Greatest Labor Saver of Modern Times

BUILT TO LAST It is well constructed, with all joints mortised, tenoned and glued under heavy pressure. All corners are angle braced, and when put together, the cabinet is perfectly rigid and will never come loose. The framework and posts are made extra heavy. The panels are built-up 3-ply construction. The back is perfectly smooth. The top section frame is made of heavy solid oak, with door frames of the same material. The door panels are 3-ply.

TOP SECTION Is white enameled on the interior. There is a 40-lb. tilting flour bin on one side, fitted with a sifter. Below the flour bin is a small compartment, fitted with a door equipped with a wire rack and holding a tea and coffee jar. On the upper right-hand side is the double compartment fitted with a shelf for holding dishes, cereals, bottles of extracts,

etc. This closes with double tight fitting doors. Below this space is another compartment, fitted with a wire rack, containing 4 glass spice jars and a swinging sugar jar. This compartment closes with a roller curtain.

You will find this roller curtain door to be a wonderful convenience as it enables you to open and close the compartment without moving the dishes and other things that you may be working with on the table top.

THE WORK TOP Can be furnished in white porcelain or shiny metal, size 25x42 in. When pulled out it gives you a working space 34x42 inches. Table top is 33 inches high from floor. Cabinet is 42 inches wide and 25 inches deep. The size is a very convenient one as it permits the cabinet being placed in almost any corner of the kitchen.

THE BASE SECTION On the upper right-hand side are two shallow drawers for kitchen cutlery and table linens. Below these two drawers is a large metal lined drawer, with sliding metal top, for keeping bread, cakes and pastries. This drawer will keep your bakery goods fresh and pure, and it is absolutely vermin-proof. Each drawer is fitted with a metal handle.

On the left-hand side is a large compartment for pots and pans. There is a wire shelf in the center fitted with a white wood bread board, both of which are removable. This compartment closes with a well fitting door equipped with a wire rack for pans, lids and shallow dishes. Cabinet is equipped with 4 easy rolling casters and stands 70 inches high over all. Shipped from factory in central Indiana. Shipping weight, about 265 lbs.

No. 34GB102. Kitchen Cabinet, complete with **$34.95** | No. 34GB103. Kitchen Cabinet, complete with porcelain **$39.95**

Cabinet Closed

KITCHEN GLASSWARE

Crystal Nested Mixing Bowls

1C1777—2 sizes, 6¼ and 7¼ in., extra deep round shape, heavy clear crystal. Asstd. 2 doz. in carton, 37 lbs.......... **Doz 95c**

1C1771—4 piece set, 5, 6, 7 and 8 in., heavy clear crystal, deep shape, smooth edges. 1 doz. sets in case, 91 lbs. **Doz sets $3.95**

5-Piece set—5, 6, 7, 8 and 9 in., deep shape, smooth edges, each set nested in carton. ½ doz. sets in shipping carton, 60 lbs.

1C1775—Clear heavy crystal.................. **Doz sets 5.75**

1C1773—Fine quality **opal glass**............. **Doz sets $8.75**

TRANSPARENT EMERALD GREEN—4 pc. set (5, 6, 7, 8 in.)
1C1768—½ doz. sets in carton................ **Doz sets $5.40**

NESTED MIXING BOWLS

Solid Red Glass

1C1767—3 pieces (9¼, 8¼ and 7¼ in.), heavy well made glass body, regulation shape, allover fired permanent solid red color, 3 nested in carton, 9 lbs. ⅓ doz. nests or more. **Doz nests $7.25**

SANITARY GLASS FOOD CONTAINER

Serves double purpose of food or butter jar and also as mixing bowl.

1C1880—6¼ in. diam., clear crystal, deep shape, sunk-in knob cover. 2 doz. in carton, 50 lbs. **Doz $1.75**

JUICE EXTRACTORS

1C2185—4 in., heavy crystal, lipped, corrugated cone, smooth edges. 3 doz. in carton, 33 lbs. **Doz 48c**

1C2186—5¾ in., extra heavy clear crystal, lipped, patent cone, improved seed catcher. 2 doz. in carton, 20 lbs. **Doz 79c**

6¼ in., heavy glass, deep saucer, paneled, seed catcher, lipped.
1C2184—Clear crystal. 2 doz. in carton, 25 lbs..... **Doz 87**
1C929—Opal glass. 3 doz. in carton, 48 lbs. **Doz 89**

1C2190—"Squeeze Easy," heavy crystal, handled, extra large saucer, sharp cone, improved seed catcher. 2 doz. in carton, 20 lbs. **Doz $1.89**

1C772—2 piece set, graduated crystal pitcher, 4⅛ in. removable reamer. 1 doz. sets in carton, 30 lbs. **Doz sets $2.75**

Lowest Prices on Beverage Bottles

Machine made bottles in clear glass.

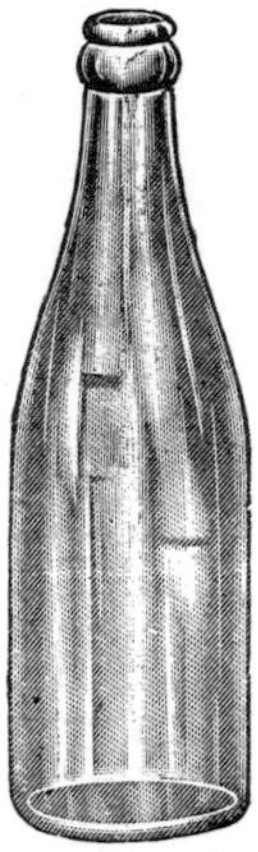

Good quality clear glass, machine made, well finished.
1C2020—Pint (8 to gal.). ¾ gro. in crate, 140 lbs. **Gro $6.00**
1C2019—Fifth (5 to gal.). ½ gro. in crate, 130 lbs. **Gro $7.25**
1C2021—Quart (4 to gal.). ½ gro. in crate, 139 lbs. **Gro $7.25**

CRYSTAL JUGS

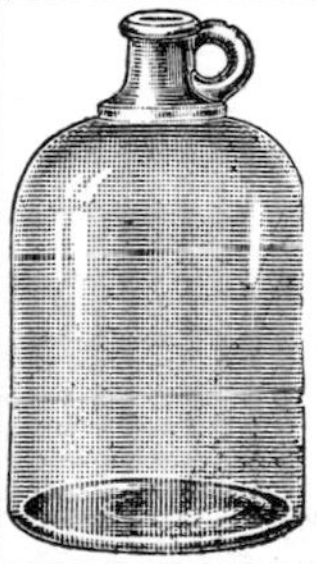

Good crystal, takes standard jug cork, glass handle.
1C2050—½ gal. 4 doz. in crate, 130 lbs. **Doz $1.25**
1C2051—1 gal. 2 doz. in crate, 107 lbs. **Doz $1.89**

FOOD CONTAINERS FOR REFRIGERATOR USE

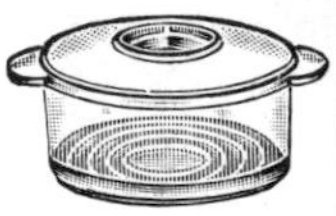

1C1981—4⅜ x 2⅛, plain crystal with 2 handles, cover with sunken lift handle. 3 doz. in carton, 60 lbs..... **Doz 92c**

1C1978—3½x4½, round, clear crystal, sunk handle. 3 doz. in carton, 53 lbs. **Doz 96c**

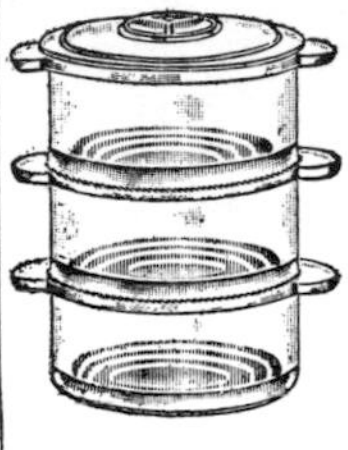

1C1877—3 piece set, three 4¾ in. deep round pressed crystal containers and 1 cover, each set in carton. ½ doz. sets in shipping carton, 25 lbs. **Doz sets $3.65**

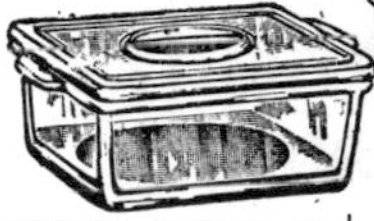

1C1982—5x4¼x2, oblong shape, good quality crystal, double handled, fitted cover with sunk-in lift. 4 doz. in case, 80 lbs..... **Doz 96c**

1C1889—2 lbs., 6x4¼, clear crystal, sunk handle, plain bottom. 1 doz. in carton, 40 lbs. **Doz $1.95**

Big Selling Butter Jar!
1C1886—1 lb., 7½ in. long, plain crystal, handled base. 2 doz. in case, 45 lbs. **Doz $1.75**

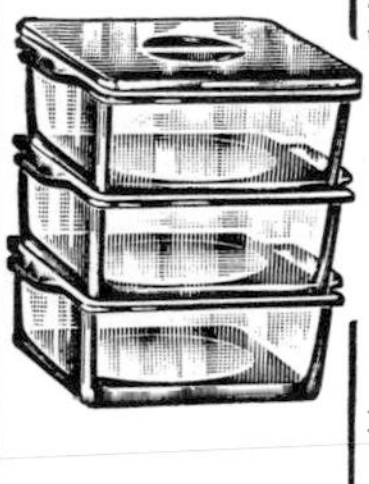

1C1882—3 piece set, 5 x 4½ x 2, pressed crystal, each set in carton. ½ doz. sets in shipping carton, 25 lbs. **Doz sets $3.85**

"3 In One" Set

1C1881—3 piece set, heavy pressed clear crystal, ONE 8¾x4¾x2¼ deep oblong tray, TWO 4¾x4¼x2⅜ covered containers which serve as cover for tray. ½ doz. sets in carton, 40 lbs........ **Doz sets $6.00**

MEASURING CUPS

1C2193 — 8 oz., 3 in. high, clear crystal, lipped, graduated forounces and pints. 2 doz. in carton, 30 lbs..... **Doz 78c**

Emerald Green

1C779—8 oz., 3½ in. high, substantial pressed **emerald green** glass, graduated for ounces and cups. 2 doz. in carton, 25 lbs. **Doz 85c**

1C2183—2 styles, plain and side lip, 8 oz., 3¼ in. high, clear crystal, graduated for ounces and cups. Asstd. 3 doz. in carton. **Doz 79c**

GLASS FUNNELS

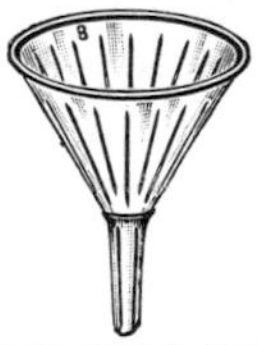

Heavy crystal, fluted inside, standard sizes.
1C61—4 oz. ½ doz. in pkg. **Doz $1.95**
1C62—8 oz. ½ doz. in pkg. **Doz $2.75**
1C63 — 16 oz. ⅓ doz. in pkg. **Doz $3.75**

"SIMPLEX" EGG BEATER

1C2182 — 1 pt., wide glass jar, lacquered screw top, double tinned wire dasher. 2 doz. in carton, 20 lbs...**Doz $1.75**

OPAL GLASS SALT BOX

1C1646—6x5½, best opal glass, embossed "Salt," hinged wood cover, wall hanger. 1 doz. in pkg., 38 lbs...**Doz $3.95**

CRYSTAL FLASKS

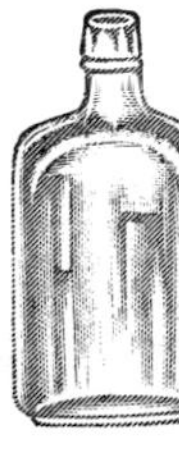

Clear crystal. 1 gro. in carton.
1C2034—½ pt. **Gro $3.40**
1C2035—1 pt. **Gro $4.95**

BEVERAGE MIXER

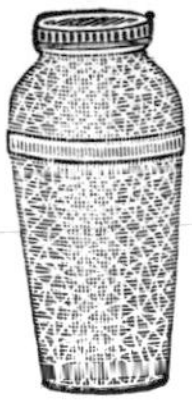

Crackled Effect Glass

1C666—8 in., 28 oz., clear finished crystal, allover crackled effect 2¼ in. wide mouth, bright red metal screw cap with leak-proof cork insert. 3 doz. in carton, 40 lbs. **Doz 96c**

BEVERAGE BOTTLE

1C2033—Quart clear crystal. ½ gro. in case. **Gro $7.50**

Our Terms **2%** TEN DAYS 1% 30 Days Net 60 Days

OPAL GLASSWARE

Is The LATEST In KITCHENWARE

Pure White . . . Heavy Pressed . . Opaque . . Smooth Finish !!

A complete line of kitchenware—especially adapted to kitchen use because it is PURE WHITE . . . it is SANITARY . . and it is DURABLE. Made under an extremely high temperature to produce strength and toughness—a mighty important feature. Keep pace with department and syndicate stores by offering this new, attractive line now. IT'S A POPULAR PRICED LINE that will appeal to every housewife who sees it in your store.

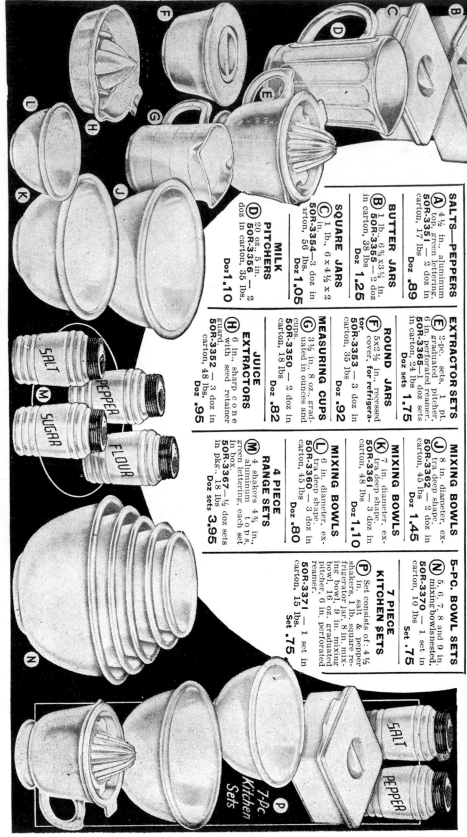

SALTS—PEPPERS

(A) 4½ in., aluminum top, green lettering. 50R-3351 — 2 doz in carton, 17 lbs **Doz .89**

BUTTER JARS

(B) 1 lb. 6⅞x3¾ in. 50R-3355 — 2 doz in carton, 38 lbs **Doz 1.25**

SQUARE JARS

(C) 1 lb. 6 x 4½ x 2 in. 50R-3354 — 3 doz in carton, 56 lbs **Doz 1.05**

MILK PITCHERS

(D) 20 oz., 5 in. 50R-3356 — 2 doz in carton, 35 lbs **Doz 1.10**

EXTRACTOR SETS

(E) 2-pc. sets, 1 pt. graduated pitcher, 6 in. perforated reamer. 50R-3365—1 doz sets in carton, 24 lbs **Doz sets 1.75**

ROUND JARS

(F) 5x2½ in. recessed cover, for refrigerator. 50R-3353 — 3 doz in carton, 35 lbs **Doz .92**

MEASURING CUPS

(G) 3½ in. 8 oz., graduated in ounces and cups. 50R-3350 — 2 doz in carton, 18 lbs **Doz .95**

JUICE EXTRACTORS

(H) 6 in. sharp cone with seed retainer guard. 50R-3352 — 3 doz in carton, 48 lbs. **Doz .82**

MIXING BOWLS

(J) 8 in. diameter, extra deep shape. 50R-3365 — 2 doz in carton, 45 lbs **Doz 1.45**

MIXING BOWLS

(K) 7 in. diameter, extra deep shape. 50R-3362 — 2 doz in carton, 48 lbs **Doz 1.10**

MIXING BOWLS

(L) 6 in. diameter, extra deep shape. 50R-3360 — 3 doz in carton, 45 lbs **Doz .80**

4 PIECE RANGE SETS

(M) 4 shakers 4¾ in. green lettering, each set in box, aluminum 4¾ in. tops, green lettering, in pkg. 18 lbs **Doz sets 3.95**

5-PC. BOWL SETS

(N) 5, 6, 7, 8 and 9 in. mixing bowls nested. 50R-3370 — 1 set in carton, 10 lbs **Set .75**

7 PIECE KITCHEN SETS

(P) Set consists of: 4½ in. salt & pepper shakers, 1 lb. square refrigerator jar, 8 in. mixing bowl, 9 in. mixing bowl, 16 oz. graduated pitcher, 6 in. perforated reamer. 50R-3371 — 1 set in carton, 15 lbs. **Set .75**

"PLATONITE" PURE WHITE GLASSWARE

With smooth edges and a fire polished finish. Made under an extremely high temperature to produce toughness, strength and heat resisting qualities "Platonite" is hard to break—it will not craze! Demonstrate its unusual durability to your customers—tell them the CUP IS ALL ONE PIECE.

Beautiful Pastel GREEN Color
"JADITE" KITCHEN GLASSWARE

RICH LOOKING JADE GREEN opalescent glass—the latest . . . the most attractive . . . the smartest line of kitchen glassware we have seen in years and years. Now for the first time, it is possible for you to sell a line like this, at popular prices. **A TRIAL ORDER OF "JADITE" will convince you it has untold sales possibilities. DON'T WAIT—ORDER NOW**—Promote this line in your community while its hot.

"JADITE" is a heavy pressed glass, finished in a dull pastel, jade green color. Every item is fire polished and full finished—truly a finish that will compel every woman to stop and marvel at its beauty. The coal black lettering adds a degree of dignity. **THE COVERS ARE RECESSED**, that is, the cover is made with a ridge around the edge to permit stacking the dishes on top of each other without danger of falling.

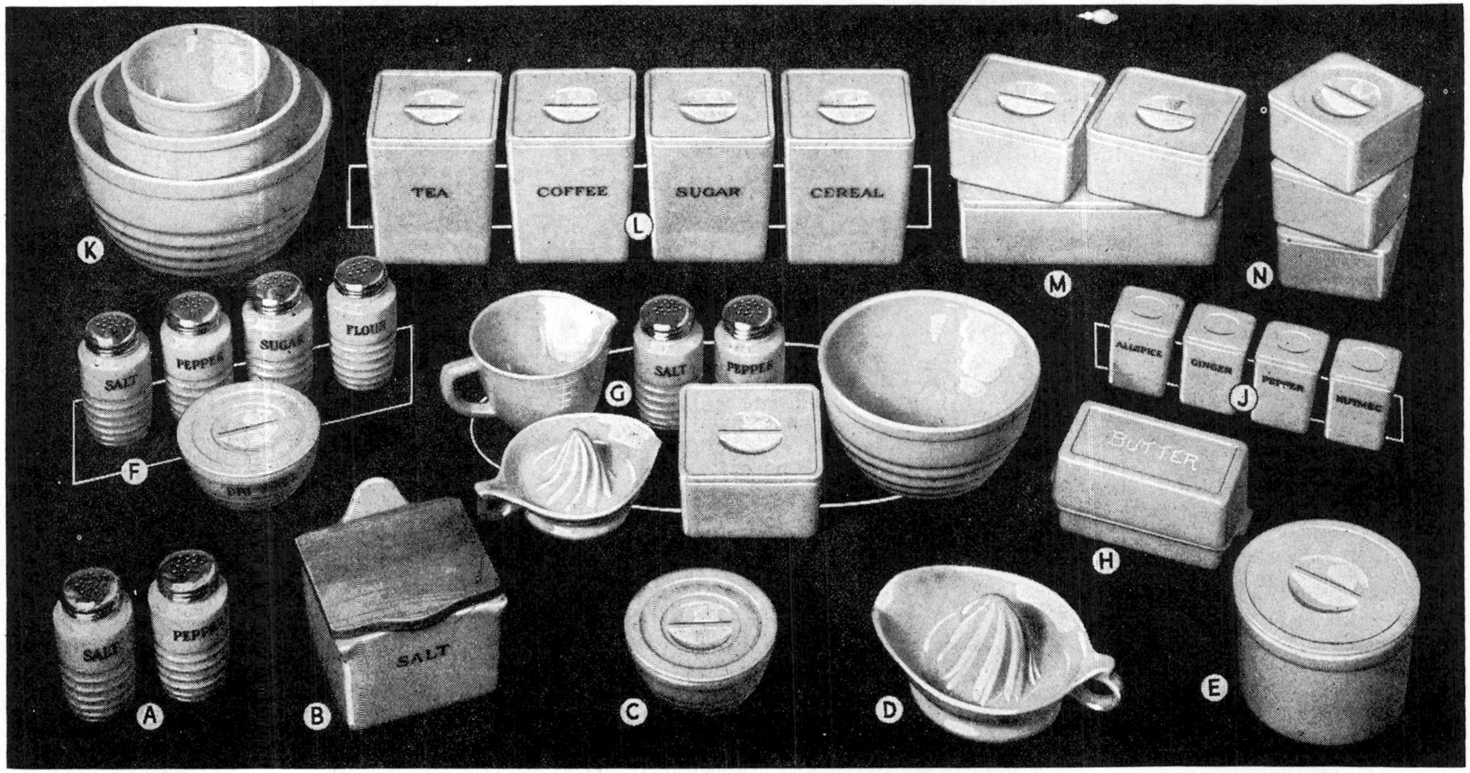

Ⓐ **Range Salt & Peppers**
4¾ in. high, polished aluminum top.
5OR-3300—2 doz. in carton, 15 lbs. . . . . Doz **1.05**

Ⓑ **Large Salt Boxes**
5½x5¼x5 in., oak finished wood cover.
5OR-3313—1 doz. in carton, 30 lbs. . . . . Doz **4.75**

Ⓒ **Refrigerator Bowls**
4¾x2⅝ in., covered.
5OR-3301—3 doz. in carton, 42 lbs. . . . . Doz **1.10**

Ⓓ **Juice Extractors**
7 in., **large size for oranges and grapefruit.**
5OR-3305—3 doz. in carton, 55 lbs. . . . . Doz **1.75**
Less quantity, Doz **1.90**

Ⓔ **Refrigerator Jars**
5¾x4¼ in., 2 lb. capacity, covered.
5OR-3307—1 doz. in carton, 30 lbs. . . . . Doz **2.25**

Ⓕ **5-Pc. Range Sets**
4 shakers, 4¾ in. high, polished aluminum tops, lettered Salt, Pepper, Sugar and Flour; **1 covered jar,** 4¾ in. diam., lettered Drippings. Each set in box.
5OR-3311—1 doz. sets in carton, 40 lbs. Doz sets **4.75**

Ⓖ **6-Pc. Kitchen Sets**
Set consists of 7½ in. deep **mixing bowl,** 4½x4½x2⅝ in. covered **refrigerator jar,** 6 in. lemon **juice extractor,** 16 oz. **measuring pitcher,** 4¾ in. **salt & pepper shakers.**
5OR-3321—1 set in carton, 9 lbs. . . . . Set **.75**

Ⓗ **Butter Jars**
6¾x3¼ in., 1 lb. capacity.
5OR-3306—2 doz. in carton, 42 lbs. . . . . Doz **2.25**

Ⓙ **4-Pc. Spice Sets**
4 jars, 3 in. high, lettered Pepper, All Spice, Nutmeg and Ginger. Each set in box.
5OR-3310—2 doz. sets in carton, 60 lbs. Doz sets **4.25**
Less quantity, Doz sets **4.50**

Ⓚ **3-Pc. Bowl Sets**
Nested 5½ in., 7½ in., and 9½ in. bowls, extra deep shape.
5OR-3322—1 set in carton, 9½ lbs. . . . . Set **.75**

Ⓛ **4-Pc. Cereal Sets**
4 jars, 4½x4½x5⅝ in., lettered Coffee, Tea, Sugar and Cereal, recessed covers.
5OR-3323—1 set in carton, 15 lbs. . . . . Set **.85**

Ⓜ **3-Pc. Refrigerator Jar Sets**
1 meat or vegetable jar, 9¾x4¾x3 in.; **2 utility jars,** 4¾x4¾x2¾ in., recessed covers.
5OR-3320—1 set in carton, 7½ lbs. . . . . Set **.69**

Ⓝ **3-Pc. Refrigerator Jar Sets**
3 jars, 4¼x4¼x2⅝ in., 1 lb. capacity, recessed covers. Each set in box.
5OR-3312—1 doz. sets in carton, 54 lbs. Doz sets **4.75**

FRY'S OVEN GLASS

The New Transparent Oven Glass

1929 PERCOLATOR TOPS   **1917 OVAL BAKER**

No.	Size	Cs. Lots	Weight	Price Per Doz.
1929	.... 2⅛	144....	60 lbs....	$2.88
1917-6	.....6⅜x4⅞x1½....	36....	31 lbs....	6.48
1917-7	.....7¼x5¼x1½....	36....	39 lbs....	7.92
1917-8	.....8¾x6¾x1½....	26....	45 lbs....	8.64

1936 CUSTARD.   **1923 RAMEKIN.**

No.	Size	Capacity	Cs. Lots	Weight	Price Doz.
1936-4½	..3½x2	....4½ oz...	72....	30 lbs..	$2.64
1936-6	..4 x2¼	..6 oz....	72....	40 lbs.	3.60
1923-4	..4 x1½	..4 oz....	72....	30 lbs..	2.88

Packed 6 in a carton

1941 ROUND BAKER OR PUDDING
Shallow Pattern.

No.	Size	Capacity	Cs. Lots	Weight	Price Per Doz.
1941-7	..7¼x2¼	..1 qt.	....24....	50 lbs.	$12.24
1941-8	..8½x2⅜	..1½ qt.	....18....	44 lbs.	14.40

1916 PIE PLATE

No.	Size	Case Lots	Weight	Price Per Doz.
1916-8	.... 8 x1⅜....	36....	58 lbs.....	$ 8.64
1916-9	.... 9 x1⅜....	36....	62 lbs.....	10.80
1916-9½	.... 9½x1½....	30....	60 lbs.....	12.24
1916-10	....10 x1¼....	24....	58 lbs.....	12.96

All Pie Plates packed 3 in a carton.

1938 ROUND CASSEROLE
Fits Standard Mountings

No.	Size	Capacity	Cs. Lots	Weight	Price Per Doz.
1938-7	..7¼x2⅝	..1 qt...	.12...	32 lbs....	$21.60
1938-8	..8¾x2¾	..1½ qt...	.12...	45 lbs....	25.20
1938-9	..9⅜x2¾	..2 qt....	. 6...	28 lbs....	28.80

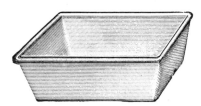

1935 SQUARE BAKER

No.	Size	Cap.	Case Lots	Wght.	Price Per Doz.
1935-8½	..8½x8½x2⅞	..2 qt...	20...	65 lbs...	$18.00

1932 OVAL CASSEROLE
Fits Standard Mountings

No.	Size	Capacity	Cs. Lots	Weight	Price Per Doz.
1932-7	..7½x5½x3½	..1½ pt...	.12...	30 lbs.	$18.00
1932-8	..8½x6¼x3	..1 qt...	.12...	34 lbs.	21.60
1932-9	..9 x7 x3⅝	..1½ qt...	.12...	50 lbs.	28.80

1922 ROUND CASSEROLE
Fits Standard Mountings

No.	Size	Capacity	Cs. Lots	Wght.	Price Per Doz.
1922-7	....7¼x3	...1 qt...	20...	60 lbs..	$21.60
1922-8	....8 x3¼	...1½ qt...	15...	60 lbs..	28.80

FRY'S OVEN GLASS

"A Dish for Every Oven Use"

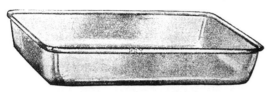

1942 UTILITY TRAY

No.	Size	Case Lots	Weight	Price Per Doz.
1942-10½	10½x6½x2	20	55 lbs.	$14.40

1939 ROUND CAKE

No.	Size	Case Lots	Weight	Price Per Doz.
1939-9	9x1¼	30	60 lbs.	$10.80

1925 ROUND SHIRRED EGG.

No.	Size	Case Lots	Weight	Price Per Doz.
1925-7	7¾x1⅝	24	40 lbs.	$10.80

1918 OVAL AU GRATIN.

No.	Size	Case Lots	Weight	Price Per Doz.
1918-8	8¾x6¾x1½	24	45 lbs.	$12.24

1918 OVAL MEAT PLATTER

No.	Size	Case Lots	Weight	Price Per Doz.
1918-13	13x9x1⅝	12	37 lbs.	$17.28

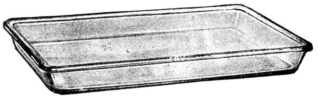

1934 BISCUIT TRAY

No.	Size	Case Lots	Weight	Price Per Doz.
1934-11	11x8½x1¼	20	60 lbs.	$14.40

1947 SQUARE CAKE

No.	Size	Case Lots	Weight	Price Per Doz.
1947-9	9¼x9¼x1½	24	51 lbs.	$14.40
1947-10	10¼x10¼x1½	12	65 lbs.	18.00

1928 BREAD BAKERS

No.	Size	Case Lots	Weight	Price Per Doz.
1928-9	9x5x3	24	56 lbs.	$12.96

No. 2005 PEARL TEA SET

Absolutely heat resisting—it will withstand extremes of temperature. Especially made vacuum handles do not carry the heat. You can pour in hot water and the handles will remain unaffected.

Each set consists of one Tea Pot and six Cups and Saucers to match. Packed in shipping carton.

Per Set

No. 2005—Pearl Tea Set, complete $12.00

KITCHEN GLASSWARE

RANGE SHAKERS—*Green*

4½ in., 8 oz., blown, perforated polished aluminum top, stippled lettering. 2 doz in carton, 13 lbs.

	Doz
50R-3200—Salt	
50R-3201—Pepper	**.52**
50R-3202—Flour	
50R-3203—Sugar	

8-PC. JAR SETS—*Green*

Just the thing for the kitchen or pantry.

Blown, polished aluminum covers, consists of **three 40 oz.** jars labeled coffee, sugar and cereal, **one 20 oz.** jar labeled tea, and **four 8 oz. shakers** labeled salt, pepper, sugar and flour.
50R-3242—1 set in carton, 8 lbs............Set **.72**

MIXING BOWLS . . . and SETS

2 Big Features

1. ROLLED EDGE—Prevents chipping and makes an easy grip for handling.
2. PANELED BASE — Permits bowls to be placed in tilted position. Heavy pressed glass.

7 in., pressed, handled and lipped. 1 doz in carton, 23 lbs.
50R-3250—Crystal
        Doz **$1.08**
50R-3251—Green
        Doz **1.25**

4-Pc. Sets—Green
5, 6, 7 and 8 in. bowls, pressed.
50R-3293—½ doz sets in carton, 44 lbs.
    Doz sets **4.50**

5-Pc. Sets—Green
5, 6, 7, 8 and 9 in. bowls, pressed.
50R-3295—1/12 doz sets in carton.
    Doz sets **6.25**

Green
Individual Sizes
Weights in order listed: 30 lbs, 40 lbs, 50 lbs, 24 lbs, 33 lbs

	In. ctn	Doz
50R-3270	5½..3..	.78
50R-3271	6½..3..	.85
50R-3272	7½..3..	1.05
50R-3273	8½..1..	1.50
50R-3274	9½..1..	1.95

5-Pc. Sets
5½, 6½, 7½, 8½ and 9½ in. bowls. 1/12 doz sets in carton, 18 lbs.
50R-3296—Green
    Doz sets **6.95**

MEASURING ITEMS

8 Oz. Cups
3¾ in., pressed, cup and ounce graduated. 2 doz in carton, 18 lbs.

	Doz
50R-3010—Crystal	.47
50R-3011—Green	.56

Pitchers
Green, pressed, graduated.
50R-3022—16 oz., 3¾ in. 1 doz in carton, 15 lbs.
    Doz **.95**
50R-3041—32 oz., 5¾ in. 1 doz in carton, 24 lbs.
    Doz **1.45**

16 Oz. Bowls
4¾ in., green, pressed, cup and pint graduated. **Also a** beater bowl.
50R-3020—1 doz in carton, 15 lbs...Doz **.89**

JUICE EXTRACTORS

Green
5½ in., pressed.
50R-3151—3 doz in carton, 25 lbs...Doz **.54**

Green
6 in., pressed.
50R-3171—3 doz in carton, 48 lbs...Doz **.87**

Green—Mammoth Size
7 in., pressed. For oranges and grapefruit.
50R-3180—3 doz in carton, 58 lbs...Doz **1.05**

2-Pc. Sets
Pressed, graduated pitcher, perforated reamer. 1 doz sets in carton.
50R-3190 — Pint, green. Wt. 25 lbs.	Doz sets **1.35**
50R-3192 — Pint, topaz. Wt. 25 lbs.	Doz sets **$1.75**
50R-3191 — Quart, green. Wt. 28 lbs.	Doz sets **1.95**

PERCOLATOR TOPS

Crystal
"Star," standard 2⅛ in.
50R-3000—1 gro in carton, 24 lbs.
    Gro **1.95**

Standard 2⅛ in. 1 gro in carton, 24 lbs.
50R-3001—Crystal
    Gro **1.95**
50R-3002—Green
    Gro **1.95**

8-PC. KITCHEN SETS

Pressed. 1 set in carton, 15 lbs.
Set consists of:
- 8 in. mixing bowl
- 9 in. mixing bowl
- 2 lb. food container
- 6x4 in. butter dish
- 3¾ in. salt shaker
- 3¾ in. pepper shaker
- 16 oz. measuring pitcher
- 5½ in. juice extractor

50R-3241—Green ....Set **.72**

WATER BOTTLES

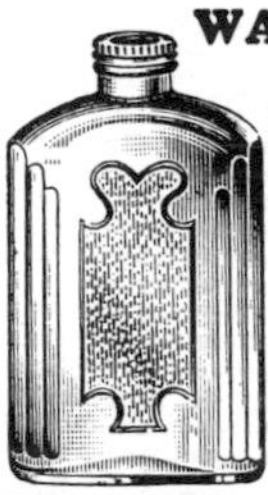

32 Oz.—Crystal
8¾ in., blown, aluminum cap.
50R-3130 — 1 doz in carton, 23 lbs.
    Doz **80c**

64 Oz.—Green
9½ in., blown, black cap.
50R-3140 — 1 doz in carton, 28 lbs.
    Doz **1.75**

32 Oz.—Green
"Tilt-Top," 7 in., blown, black cap.
50R-3131—1 doz in carton, 23 lbs.
    Doz **.89**

FOOD JARS FOR REFRIGERATORS

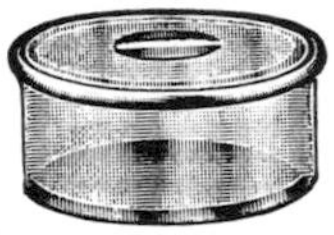

5¾ x 2¾ in., 1 lb., pressed. 2 doz in carton, 45 lbs.
50R-3050—Crystal
    Doz **.95**
50R-3051—Green
    Doz **1.05**

5x4¼ in., 1 lb., pressed. 3 doz in case, 50 lbs.
50R-3054—Crystal
    Doz **.95**
50R-3055—Green
    Doz **1.05**

6¾ x3¼ in., 1 lb., pressed. 2 doz in carton, 50 lbs.
50R-3070—Crystal **1.10**
50R-3071—Green **1.15**

6-Pc. Sets—Crystal
It revolves—a flip of the finger brings the container to you.
Five 1 quart triangular shaped covered glass jars. 11¼ in. diam. ball bearing white enameled stand.
50R-3121—1 set in carton, 14 lbs................Set **1.35**

3-Pc. Sets—Topaz
Each jar 5¼ x2 in., cover fits all 3 jars, pressed. Each set in box.
50R-3102—½ doz sets in carton, 25 lbs.
    Doz sets **$3.75**

4-Pc. Sets—Green
Panel design, **cover on each jar**, 1 jar 8½x8½x3 in., 1 jar 8½x4¼x3 in., 2 jars 4⅛x4⅛x2 in., pressed.
50R-3112—1 set in carton, 10 lbs...Set **.75**

TABLE GLASSWARE

MATCHED TABLEWARE

GREEN ... Colonial Block
Pattern ... Heavy Pressed

4 In. Creamers
50R-3610—3 doz in carton, 30 lbs. Doz .84

6 In. Sugar Bowls
50R-3612—3 doz in carton, 48 lbs. Doz .92

4¾ In. Butter Dishes
May be used for jelly or preserves.
50R-3611—3 doz in carton, 38 lbs. Doz .85

6¾ In. Butter Dishes
50R-3613—3 doz in carton, 62 lbs. Doz .92

BERRY BOWLS—NAPPIES

POPULAR DESIGNS ... pressed glass ... deep shapes.

GREEN—Block Design—Star Bottoms
7 In. Berry Bowls
50R-3920—3 doz in carton, 50 lbs. Doz .89

4½ In. Nappies
50R-3900—6 doz in carton, 35 lbs. Doz .38

GREEN—Process Etched "Florentine" design
8 In. Berry Bowls
50R-3921—2 doz in carton, 32 lbs. Doz .95

4½ In. Nappies
50R-3911—6 doz in carton, 28 lbs. Doz .39

8½ In. Berry Bowls
"Sierra" panel design, extra deep shape. 4 doz in carton, 60 lbs
50R-3924—Green
50R-3925—Rose-pink Doz .92

8 In. Berry Bowls
"Adam" design, process etched floral design, fluted pattern. 4 doz in carton, 62 lbs
50R-3927—Rose-pink
50R-3926—Green Doz 1.05

4 In. Nappies
Process-etched clover leaf border. 6 doz in carton, 26 lbs.
50R-1096—Green Doz .25

SYRUP PITCHERS

Green
12 oz., 6¼ in., blown, removable metal top.
50R-3550—2 doz in carton, 26 lbs. Doz 1.25

Crystal
9½ oz. 4¾ in., pressed, optic fluted, removable metal top.
50R-3551—2 doz in carton, 20 lbs. Doz 1.35

Crystal
15 oz., 6⅛ in., pressed prism fluted, removable metal top.
50R-3560—1 doz in carton, 17 lbs. Doz 2.15

VINEGAR OR OIL BOTTLES

Crystal
8 oz., 6 in., pressed.
50R-3570—2 doz in carton, 20 lbs. Doz .80

Crystal
6 oz., 5¾ in., blown.
50R-3572—2 doz in carton, 15 lbs. Doz .89

Asstd. Crystal & Green
5 oz., 6¾ in., pot glass.
50R-3590—1 doz in carton, 12 lbs. Doz 2.15

CEREAL DISHES

5 in., extra deep, light pressed, process-etched clover leaf border. 4 doz in carton, 25 lbs.
50R-1037—Topaz Doz .39

SALAD PLATES

8 in., pressed, process etched clover leaf border.
50R-1091—3 doz in carton, 33 lbs. Doz .60

SUGARS, CREAMERS AND SETS

3¾ in., pressed, process-etched clover leaf border. 3 doz in carton, 17 lbs.
SUGARS—
50R-1094—Green Doz .36
CREAMERS—
50R-1093—Green Doz .36

Sugar & Creamer Sets
Sugar and creamer 3½ in., pressed. 24 lbs. Doz sets 80c

CAKE PLATES

Green
10¼ in., pressed, dewdrop design, embossed floral and leaf border.
50R-3985—1 doz in carton, 25 lbs. Doz 2.25

SALT & PEPPER SHAKERS

Crystal
3¾ in., concave panels, metal top.
50R-3506—3 doz in box, 7 lbs. Doz .36

Green
3 in., modernistic design, aluminum top.
50R-3504—3 doz in carton, 10 lbs. Doz .42

Crystal
4¾ in., nickeled top.
50R-3531—2 doz in case, 10 lbs. Doz .79

Green
3¾ in., chromium plated top.
50R-3506—4 doz in carton, 15 lbs. Doz .45

MISCELLANEOUS ITEMS

Tooth Pick Holders
2¾ x 2¾ in., thin blown crystal, genuine cut.
50-3730—1 doz in box Doz .78

Opal Glass Mugs
3½ in., heavy opal glass.
50R-3733—3 doz in carton, 40 lbs. Doz .85

Egg Cups
4½ in., double deck, heavy pressed crystal.
50R-3732—2 doz in carton, 18 lbs. Doz .87

Milk Pitchers
20 oz., 5 in., green, pressed.
50R-3673—2 doz in carton, 30 lbs. Doz .92

GREEN 7-PC. BERRY SETS

8 in. bowl, 6 nappies 4¾ in., pressed, deep shape, imitation cut.
50R-3990—½ doz sets in carton, 25 lbs. Doz sets 3.95

BUTLER BROTHERS

Additional Books By Gene Florence

Collectors Encyclopedia of Depression Glass	**$14.95**
Pocket Guide to Depression Glass	**$ 8.95**
Collectors Encyclopedia of Occupied Japan II	**$12.95**

Add $1.00 postage for the first book, $.35 for each additional book.

Copies of these books may be ordered from:

Gene Florence
P.O. Box 22186
Lexington, KY 40522

or

COLLECTOR BOOKS
P.O. Box 3009
Paducah, KY 42001